Also by Leonard Wibberley

Stranger at Killnock
The Quest of Excalibur
Beware of the Mouse
Take Me to Your President
McGillicuddy McGotham
The Mouse That Roared
Mrs. Searwood's Secret Weapon
The Mouse on the Moon
A Feast of Freedom
The Island of the Angels
The Hands of Cormac Joyce
The Road from Toomi
Adventures of an Elephant Boy
The Mouse on Wall Street

NONFICTION

Ah Julian!
Yesterday's Land
Towards a Distant Island
No Garlic in the Soup
The Land That Isn't There

JUVENILES *(Fiction)*

Peter Treegate's War
Kevin O'Connor and the Light Brigade
The Wound of Peter Wayne
John Treegate's Musket
Deadmen's Cave
Sea Captain from Salem

JUVENILES *(Nonfiction)*

Wes Powell—Conqueror of the Colorado
The Life of Winston Churchill
John Barry—Father of the Navy
The Epics of Everest
Man of Liberty—the Life of Thomas Jefferson

Voyage by Bus

By LEONARD WIBBERLEY

 *William Morrow and Company, Inc.*

NEW YORK • 1971

Printed in the United States of America

Library of Congress Catalog Card Number 78-128785

Voyage by Bus

chapter
One

I AM by nature a voyager, though mere traveling I find the dullest of pastimes. You will immediately appreciate the difference. The traveler goes from place to place using scheduled transportation and along routes established by another who takes the responsibility for getting him there. The voyager sets out on his own, chooses his own route, stops where he pleases, makes side trips on a whim and lives, rather than endures, his journey.

Voyaging is plainly preferable and I have spent the past several summers voyaging, though largely upon the ocean. Then came one summer when I decided to try a voyage by land; an exploration of the American West, in a land yacht, navigating by charts provided by gas stations, with an occasional glance perhaps at Polaris or Antares to be sure that the maps knew what they were talking about. (One should never be parted from the stars. A glance at them will give you not only direction but comfort.)

Land yachts are available these days in fair quantity though they are called many names. Mobile homes are the biggest of them, the equivalent perhaps of large schooners. Then there are vast trailers, pulled by the family car, and sleeping four, five or six, which I will liken to schooners and ketches not having inboard power but requiring to be towed by tugs from place to place. After them come campers–little sloops and cutters–sleeping four adults perhaps, and handy both for traveling and for running in and out of little coves with which the country abounds. These are the most numerous of the land craft, and they journey from shore to shore and border to border across the continent in every kind of weather. When you pass one on the highway, rocking a bit perhaps in a cross-wind, give it room and a kind word, for its home port may be two or three thousand miles away, and the captain and mate, companions of forty years and more.

Before any decision could be made on my own projected voyage, however, I first opened the subject to my family at Sunday dinner. "This summer," I said, eying my son Coco, who was about to upset a glass of milk, "I thought we might all go on a voyage together."

Patricia, my eldest daughter (she is eighteen), gave Hazel, her mother, a glance of holy resignation. She is a very brave girl and has suffered through many voyages to the offshore islands of California, being prone to seasickness. Arabella, who is thirteen and of independent mind, said firmly, "Good-bye." Kevin, aged twenty, my eldest son, and Christopher, seventeen, looked concerned. Kevin has three times sailed to Hawaii with me and Christopher once, and they had other plans. Rory, who will make a fine seaman soon, was excited and so also was Coco, who upset his milk.

"I'm talking of a land voyage," I said. "A voyage through the western parts of America in a bus fitted up like a yacht. With bunks for everybody and a gas stove to cook on, and lots of places for clothes and no water coming through the deck or portholes, and even a shower bath."

There was a slight stirring of interest, but no huzzas except from Rory and Coco, who are enthusiastic about everything, not having lived long enough to be otherwise. "We can travel through forests and through deserts, along mountain passes over valleys and see mountain meadows twenty miles in extent," I said. "We can camp by the sea or by solitary lakes and see deer and bear and moose. Once your mother and I saw a moose in Yellowstone. It was the biggest thing we ever saw. A moose at close quarters dwarfs the Empire State Building."

"Real bears?" asked Arabella.

"Yes. Real live bears. Black ones and brown ones."

"What about the cats?" asked Arabella, who is so partial to cats that we have three of them—Hermith, Pancho, and a kitten, Tich. They are all different colors and all related.

"We can get someone to look after Hermith and Pancho," I said.

"We can take the kitten," said Kevin. It is really his kitten. He had one on the boat—Motley, a seafaring kitten of dash and charm that used to go swimming in the warm water of Lahaina Harbor, Maui, in the Hawaiian Islands.

By degrees the voyage was agreed upon, the conversation swinging from the trivial to the magnificent as is the case in all such discussions. We would see the Grand Canyon and the Big Sur country, the Painted Desert and the Cascade Mountains, the smoking coasts of Oregon and the sacred city of the Apaches. We would be sure to tell the milkman not to leave any milk, and the gardener to water my roses.

It was not hard to find a vessel for the voyage. There were plenty of them advertised in the classified section of the *Los*

Angeles Times, and I picked at random the Santa Monica Motor Home Rentals, Inc., which was not too far away.

Mr. Paul Ricard, owner of the company, took us into a yard at the back of his premises and there we saw what looked like two small Greyhound buses. One had a red line around its white sides, and the other a blue line. I liked the red line.

"Let's look at the red one," I said, and Mr. Ricard agreed immediately. It was entered by a step which folded down from the front door, which will give you an idea of how high the bus stood off the road. If you ignored the steering wheel up forward it was remarkably like a modern yacht on the inside, so much so that I immediately felt at home.

On the left side was the driver's seat, with the wheel before him and the gearshift on his right side. He sat beside the engine and over his own left front wheel which gave exceptional visibility. On the side opposite him was another seat for a copilot, map reader and sandwich passer. Driver and copilot were on a little ledge or dais above the general level of the floor or cabin sole, giving each of them an enjoyable feeling of command and slight superiority.

Behind these two seats stretched the whole luxury of the bus, which was carpeted throughout and had also a transparent thick plastic cover over much of the carpeting—a very sensible precaution. If you will imagine yourself looking aft or backwards along the bus, these are the arrangements. To your right a comfortable sofa of ample proportions. The seat of this made one bed at night. The back, splendidly padded, lifted up on a hinge from the seat and fastened to the ceiling by stout straps, providing another bed. So by day on that side was a sofa and by night two single beds.

Opposite this sofa was a dinette, that is to say, two seats facing each other with a table between them. Two adults could readily sit in each seat. At nighttime the table was taken out, the seats bent flat and moved so that they touched, and in this position, they provided a comfortable double bed for two children. Over the top of this, on a bracket from the wall, a light camp cot with an aluminum frame could be suspended, providing a further single bed.

Continuing aft past the sofa on your right was a galley—a four-burner stove utilizing butane, with oven, a sink with a formica worktable over the top, cupboards above and storage below. Very tidy and easy to clean and operate. Under the sink was a contrivance for heating the bus. With great patience Mr. Ricard showed me how to use it. There are people who can work these things, but I am not one of them. I have a fear of gas in enclosed places and so I did not use the heater, and we did not need it.

Opposite the galley was a generous hanging closet with an air-conditioning unit over the top of it—another unit of smaller capacity being located in the ceiling forward. The closet also contained the controls for the air-conditioning unit and for the electrical current in the bus—a tape recorder forward over the driver's seat and the interior lights. Again, looking astern, there was on the righthand side the "head"—that is, toilet and washbasin with a small hand-held device for taking a shower. Beyond this was a double bed lying across the back of the bus. This was a very comfortable double bed indeed, and beside it, at the foot, was a chest of drawers, which Hazel later divided up among the children.

But this is not all. Beneath the double bed in the back of the bus was more storage space and a heater for hot water. And I forgot to mention that on the same side as the hanging closet and opposite the stove was a small but ample refrigerator that really worked, though it would turn off if the bus was not level when parked. There was more yet. Outside, in a small compartment of its own, was a gasoline-driven generator, so that between the generator on the engine and the auxiliary generator, there was no question whatever of batteries running down, however much current we might use.

It was truly a well-appointed bus. It had water tanks holding fifty gallons and these were pressurized so that the water rushed out of the faucet as soon as it was turned on. Over the workspace by the sink was a gauge which showed how much water was in the tanks.

If you have been counting beds and people you will see that there were beds for seven, but there would be eight of us aboard. This we decided to solve by putting Rory and Cormac (Coco)—who together would weigh only as much as an adult—in the camp cot over the dinette at nights.

We rented the bus there and then for a month and went home delighted to tell the children that the land voyage was arranged and to wait out the days remaining until they were all out of school.

chapter

Two

The plan was to go up the Pacific Coast Highway and then follow California State Highway 1 through the Big Sur country to Monterey, for here some of the loveliest coast in the world is to be seen. Also State Highway 1 is what a wanderer's road should be—it meanders here and there, following the indentation of the coast line, crosses ravines, climbs hills, plunges out into the sunlight on bold cliffs and then slides down into valleys shaded by redwoods and pines and soft with verdant ferns and grasses.

I had mentioned this plan to the children, pointed out that we would be at all times close to the sea (for the sea is our great love) and we should also have some splendid views of it. I hinted that there might be opportunities to surf, a sport which Kevin and Rory dote on. And we might do what I have always avoided doing—stop at Hearst's great castle and make a tour of the place. It is now a place of legends, haunted by the great gaunt figure of William Randolph Hearst, who, it is said, despoiled half of Europe to furnish it with knick-knacks.

This was a very fine plan and it lasted from the door of our house to the juncture of our road with Pacific Coast Highway, which is scarcely a tenth of a mile away. When we got there, waiting for the traffic lights, the plan changed. Instead of turning left up Pacific Coast Highway, I crossed the road to head inland.

"Where are you going?" demanded Kevin, who had taken the copilot seat beside me.

"Death Valley," I said.

"That's a long way from Big Sur."

"It is," I replied. "But I think we should go to Death Valley and then to the Grand Canyon and then to the Dinosaur National Monument and we'll find out what happens after that."

The decision was not as capricious as it seems. Neither Kevin nor Christopher had seen any of these places and they could not stay with us for the whole voyage but had to return to Hermosa Beach—Kevin to work and Christopher to start practice for the fall high school football season. The Big Sur country we had already seen together.

"Death Valley at this time of the year is going to be unbearable," said Hazel, who is from Arizona and knows about desert heat. But I, being from Ireland, tend to temper all climates to that which prevails in my own land, and did not believe, however hot Death Valley got, that it would be insufferable. And so, the decision made, we plunged east instead of north.

The week before we started out Mr. Ricard had given both Hazel and me driving lessons with the bus. The main difficulty lay in gauging the size of the thing. It was twenty-seven feet long, but had a short wheel base, so that it could turn corners in something close to the radius of a large car. The width was the hardest dimension to get used to. The bus was a good two feet wider than the family car with the result that I came within inches of sideswiping cars parked by the side of the street until I grew accustomed to the unusual beam.

The best thing to do was to drive by the center line on the road. Even that called for a readjustment, for the driver's seat was over the front wheel. Glancing at the center line, one got the impression that the bus was very close to it, though actually it was five or six feet away. It took positive determination to ease out farther toward the middle of the road and so avoid swiping cars parked on your right. Once this peculiarity was mastered, however, the bus proved quite as easy to drive as a car. It was also big enough to receive a certain deference from other traffic though the body, I found, was made of fiber glass.

Getting out of Los Angeles is very easy. You just select your freeway and go, but it is well to bear in mind that the rule for freeway driving is almost exactly the opposite of the rule for driving on roads. In short, when you change lanes, you must speed up and not slow down or you will likely get rammed from the rear. In our case, headed for Death Valley, we took the San Bernadino freeway eastwards and then, clear of the city, turned north out onto the vast Mojave Desert, which is the first of that tremendous series of deserts extending south, east, and north to Mexico, Texas, and Colorado, and once known as The Great American Desert.

We had started late in the day and this first day's run was likely to be short. We could not expect to do much more than get free of the city, out into the clean desert air, and then find somewhere to park for the night. But once we were out in the Mojave and had got off the freeway onto a side road heading in the general direction of Death Valley, the mysterious presence of the desert lured us on and on, mile after mile. It is strange, indeed, how much variety there is in both ocean and desert where the general impression is one of constant sameness.

The Mojave Desert is not of sand but of dried mud in which there are very many small stones—conglomerate is the geologist's term (one which I think Wall Street has borrowed from them). The floor of the desert, undulating slightly, is pierced on every horizon by jagged peaks, serrated, sharp, with deep gulleys worn into them and ridges running down their flanks boldly to the desert floor and seemingly plunging down deep below it.

These mountains are actually drowning in their own debris. All that we see of them is the eroded heads. Wind, rain, sun, and frost have crumbled them to fine mud and little stones, which flow down their sides to form the desert floor. The desert floor is being added to year by year, the geologists say, and will finally rise until it covers the tops of the very mountains from which it came, which will then be submerged completely in the product of their own decay.

What a strange landscape it is, once you have the elements of the story—that flat, rising sea of dried mud and thrusting desperately above it the peaks of the mountains frantic to survive. These peaks are colored in pastel shades—pale grays and blues and pinks. Only at dawn and at dusk are there strong colors on the desert. The rest of the day the bright light, diffused through billions of dust particles, thins all colors to mere shades. And at night the desert disappears into darkness and it is the sky which comes alive, shining down upon the nothingness of earth.

Originally the mountains which formed the desert were

eroded by tremendous rains but now it is the wind which rubs them down. And the wind was at work as the sun set that day, a roaring westerly of twenty knots or perhaps more, carrying with it the sting of sand and causing the bus to shake and sway as I cut across it, headed north for Death Valley. I was surprised at the amount of windage the bus offered, and how it rolled and got a skittish feeling in the gusts.

When the sun had gone and the desert twilight was over, I realized that I had journeyed too long for the first day and that in the dark I would have a problem finding a place to park for the night. On the surface, the problem of parking seemed easy to solve. All that was needed, surely, was to pull off the road onto the desert. But I now discovered that there was a deep drainage gully running along both sides of the road which the bus could not cross. And when I found a place at which the gully could be crossed, Kevin reported that the desert surface on the other side was too soft to bear the weight of the bus.

The road plunged on straight and narrow, headed for the Wildrose entrance to Death Valley. The wind rose higher. The desert seemed endless and offered no harbor. And then at last Kevin found a narrow channel, as it were, leading off the road between two slight hills like a harbor mole. We stopped the bus and walked over the ground and solemnly assured each other that it was firm and would hold the weight of the bus. Then I backed up and pulled slowly in to find ahead a nice flat area under the lee of the little hills.

While Hazel and Patricia got the beds ready (we had stopped for dinner in a small town before turning off into the desert) I went outside to look about. The wind was warm and dust-dry and made a low boom as it fled between the little hills behind which we had sheltered the bus. It was up to

chapter
Three

THE wind rose mightily in the small hours of the morning, buffeting the bus so that it rocked even under the lee of the little hills. I listened to the hiss of it in the blackness of the night and the little whimper it made here and there on the corners. It had gone round a point or two to the north so that the bus no longer had her stern to it. I wondered, lying snug in bed, whether I should not start the engine and head her into the weather so that she would lie more quietly. I have often had to do a similar thing when sailing—wake up in the middle of the night uneasy over the boat's motion and go on deck to let out more scope on the anchor so the boat could ride more easily in the wind and sea.

But now I considered that I was after all on land and that if I started the engine it would wake the children and also that Kevin would think I was fussing. He has come to think of me as fussing, for the great difference between twenty and fifty is that twenty does not care and fifty cares too much. I tend to fuss now—to check whether doors are really locked and lights turned off and faucets too. It is sad, for there was a time, when I was Kevin's age, when I would have headed for Singapore without even stopping to put on a hat.

So I lay in the dark for a while, listening to the wind and debating moving the bus, and finally I found that using Kevin and the children as an excuse, I could lie in bed and do nothing about it, which is exactly what I did. The wind dropped a little and I fell asleep and did not awake again until full daylight.

Nobody, to tell the truth, had rested very well that night but we had a good breakfast and made the bus tidy and I took my little sons, Rory and Cormac, for a walk on the desert to show them what it is like when you look at it very closely and do not take in the grand view. I thought I might find for them a fossil sea shell, for in late Ordovician times, this whole area lay under the sea and, indeed, in Baja California to the south there is a valley whose bed is sheathed with fossil shells. But the desert was, as I have said, a vast dried-up mudslide, great deltas and fans of mud having slipped down from the mountains all around to make the desert floor. Indeed on the other side of the low range of mountains that now stretched between us and the ocean, people build expensive homes on this million-year-old mudslide, and when there are heavy rains in Southern California, their houses slide into the roads or down into other people's houses, to the entertainment of the rest of the nation. A friend of mine awoke one morning after a night of rain to find his swimming pool lying across the highway below, a huge concrete bowl with the diving board still attached. Not only had he lost his essential symbol of success, but the highway department sent him a vast bill for breaking it up and carting it away, proving that when the mighty have fallen everybody takes a kick at them.

There are mudslides every year in the Los Angeles area

but such are the persuasive talents of the real estate salesmen (descendants perhaps of those who sold building lots on the flanks of Pompeii) that the building goes on and on, and people vie with each other to build homes on a little niche cut into a massive mudpile from which, on a clear day, they may see the ocean.

If you should travel Pacific Coast Highway northward past Santa Monica, you can see the thickness of that ancient river of mud dramatically displayed. It is a hundred feet high or so, rising in cliffs above the highway and called Pacific Palisades. The cliffs are all mud and on top of them are the former homes of movie stars. Some now totter on the edge of the cliffs, which have been worn away by wind and by rain. Walkways around what were once pleasant lawns now jut into the empty air, and it is only a few years ago that four ladies, playing a hand of bridge in a little Chinese pagoda on the top of these cliffs, were hurtled to the bottom when the cliff gave way beneath them. (No one was seriously hurt and the bid at that moment was, I believe, a rather risky "Two No Trumps.")

A thousand vast mudslides are to be found, then, throughout Southern California and the mud at the place we had camped for the night had traveled a long way, for the small pebbles in it were lacking sharp corners. There was a thin growth on the desert despite the summer drought—not the creosote bushes and sage, which is found all about, but a spindly plant putting out a tiny mustard-yellow flower with leaves like pale-green sticks. Ghostly lizards skittered across our path so fast that all that was visible of them was the disturbed dust of their passage. Lacking fossils, Rory and Coco each found an empty .22 rifle shell and were more pleased with these than any fossil I might have provided.

We traveled toward Death Valley on State Highway 178

with the mauve and blue Panamint mountains ahead of us. Seen from a distance, the Panamints have as much and no more reality than the mountains on a stage backdrop, and although they are quite high—Telescope Peak, for instance, has an elevation of eleven thousand feet—the vast desert space makes them seem but a low fringe of hills. Our road, on reaching them, moved parallel with the spine of the range, winding and twisting about, now thrusting in and now being rebuffed, and climbing a little all the while until at last with a tremendous rush to the east, it found a passage through the mountains.

Death Valley announced its approach somewhat grimly. By the side of the road we came up on a fifty-gallon drum, mounted on a stout bracket and containing water. It was provided by the National Park Service and this water was not for drinking but for refilling radiators, for it is failing automobiles and not failing oxen which are the hazards in crossing Death Valley today. The hazard is real. Indeed, only a month before we made our crossing a family of three died when their car stalled because of a vapor lock in the gas line. They had set out to look for water and died of exposure.

With the tank of water was a leaflet giving some hints on survival in this the hottest part of the United States. Some were obvious—like wearing a hat and a shirt in the sun, and not straying any from the main roads. Some were not obvious and all the more useful for that reason. Grades, for instance, the leaflet said, are deceptive in the open space of the desert and the brighter light. What seems to be flat ground may actually be a hill. It is better then to change down than to "lug" your engine. If the engine boils over it is advisable to turn the car around and face the wind and run the engine to cool it. If the engine does stall, stay with the car.

We read these instructions solemnly, checked the water level in the radiator, and, feeling a little shaken, moved up the pass into the valley. The sun was now high and the heat and glare grew worse and worse. The road also deteriorated. First it was full of potholes. Then there were places where the surface had been repaired with stones which had not yet been rolled. Then, though not yet in the valley, we came to a place where the road disappeared altogether. I stopped the bus and looked about. Ahead was what looked like a dry riverbed; boulders and sand lay on every side, giving every evidence of having been brought there by floodwater.

"There's the road," said Kevin. "Up there." He pointed over to the left and there, sure enough, was the road, washed a hundred feet away by the floods caused by the rain of the previous spring. Biblical floods they must have been, with the whole Panamint range of mountains a watershed and only the deep canyons between to carry away the deluge. The road was washed out not in one, but in a dozen places, and it appeared that a whole encampment of trailers had been caught in that mighty spring flood of a few months previous, and carried off in the general direction of Mexico. For ourselves, I put the bus in its lowest gear and bounced and crashed over this washed-out road, avoiding boulders and soft sand until I got back onto a patch of asphalt surface.

We were entering Death Valley by Emigrant Pass, and we staggered along at three or four miles an hour raising a mighty cloud of dust. The day grew hotter, the road got worse and the temperature in the bus rose higher and higher.

At this point there arose a mild dispute between Hazel and me about the air-conditioning system. Hazel was of the opinion that it would be cooler in the bus if we turned off one of the air-conditioning units. I said that this was nonsense. I said that this was the equivalent of saying that two plus two equaled nothing. I said this very politely and at the same time told Kevin (who had relieved me at the wheel) to steer a trifle to port, for the Rock of Gibraltar's little brother was lying at the bottom of a gulley on the starboard side. Kevin avoided the Rock of Gibraltar's little brother, but got into some soft sand which called for some delicate work with the accelerator before we were through. In the meantime the interior of the bus got a trifle cooler.

"What did you do?" I asked, feeling the slightest breath of cool air on my neck.

"I turned one of the air conditioners off," Hazel replied. Half an hour later and one mile down the road I figured that Hazel had actually turned the air conditioner "on" and that it had been "off" before. I drifted to the rear of the bus and to the switch that operated the air conditioner there—the big one. The switch was in a dark part of the closet, behind some clothes, and without my glasses I couldn't see whether it was on or off. I flipped it anyway. The bus immediately got warmer.

I got my glasses and examined the switch. Where it stood right then the switch was "on." And the bus was hot. I turned it to "off"—the bus got cooler. I do not pretend to understand this. Not everything in the world is answerable to human reason. I left the switches where they were and went back to spot boulders for Kevin.

"Figure it out?" he asked.

"No," I said. "But your mother could make a fortune in the air-conditioning business."

For over an hour we struggled along the pass with the washed-out road, more often more of a dry riverbed than a roadway, and at last gained the west door of the valley at

Stove Pipe Wells. We stopped for a moment to look the valley over. It stretched before us, flat and scintillating to a distant range of mountains and north and south to the horizon. It seemed, even in this modern bus, a place of menace, a place where a quite trivial accident might endanger us all. Here and there a dust devil danced across the valley floor and the little asphalt-surfaced road was soon lost in the bright heat of the distance. It was lonely and repelling and I was not quite at ease as I slipped the bus into gear and moved off into it.

chapter

Four

DEATH VALLEY has many aspects and one of them is of a Barnum and Bailey sideshow character, with one incongruity piled upon another. It is, for instance, the driest part of the United States, but at least one of its victims died of drowning. His body was found by a surveyor in 1895. It had been washed by a flash flood into a canyon. A letter in the dead man's pocket gave his name as Titus. He has his monument in Titus Canyon, which was named after him.

Again there is in Death Valley a golf course and a castle, and a swimming pool. The golf course and swimming pool are part of the equipment of the Furnace Creek Inn, located near the spot where in 1849 a starving, parched band of immigrants camped on their way to the California goldfields. Children play happily in the ice-clear waters of the pool where a few generations earlier others died of thirst.

There are fish in Death Valley—inch-long pupfish which thrive in Salt Creek, which is the only river that flows all through the valley; others appear and disappear. Its water is undrinkable and the fish are descendants of schools that flourished in the long-gone inland sea that once occupied the place. It is said that sardines, pickled in brine, are to be found in parts of the valley and they are the favorite food of coyotes, and this may well be true.

Broiled ducks are at times found on the salt flats. These, migrating across the valley, are caught in the furnace blast of hot air which rises from it, and fall exhausted to the ground to be broiled, feathers and all, in the sun.

In the salt of the valley too are the tracks of prehistoric camels and elephants. There is certainly a castle in Death Valley—Scotty's Castle at the northern end, built for an eccentric prospector, Walter Scott, by an equally eccentric insurance millionaire, Albert Johnson. There is an incongruity even in that partnership—a desert prospector and a Chicago millionaire, who poured more than a million dollars into building him a castle, all the time pretending that the money came from a mysterious gold mine the prospector had discovered.

There must be a good thousand stories of Death Valley Scotty, all belonging to that vein of humor that is peculiarly American—The Tall Tale. Some can be readily dismissed as fictitious. Of others there is a lingering doubt because of the character of the man. I give you one. During his life as a prospector, Scotty several times lent food, blankets, and other equipment to a man who was so mean that he never paid back these debts. Not only that, he would never lend anything to another or if he did, only to make outrageous demands in return. Eventually this man died, his debts unpaid and his reputation for meanness unimpaired. News of his death was brought to Scotty, who to everybody's surprise said he would underwrite all the costs of the funeral and took possession of the body.

"What did you do with him?" he was asked.

"Well," said Scotty, "I gave him the kind of send-off he deserved. I put him in a pine coffin and mailed him to his family back East—COD."

So the extravagant tales of Death Valley mount but they are only one aspect of this vast valley and in all, a small one. Far greater an aspect is the air of menace, of desolation and of the forbidden which looms over the whole place. As we moved off across its floor, and as the interior of the bus, despite the air conditioning, became hotter and hotter, the brooding threat of the place increased. Lonely, burned out, and empty, the landscape seemed not to belong to Earth but to some planet forbidden to man.

Death Valley was named by the survivors of a party who entered it on Christmas Day, 1849, on their way to the California goldfields. The promise of gold spurred them to look for a faster route to California than the old Spanish trail. They fell for the story of a secret map showing a quick route to the goldfields and, leaving the main party on the Spanish Trail to the north, headed south. There was no map and they were soon lost and split up into several sub-parties—the Jayhawkers comprising about twenty wagons from Illinois, and the Georgians and Mississippi Boys, the Manley-Bennett party and the Brier family. At times these various parties traveled together. At times they separated either by consent or by happenstance.

Twenty-seven wagons in all lumbered into the valley on Christmas Day, 1849, on creaking, sun-dried wheels for there had been no grease for the axles since leaving Utah. They camped at Furnace Creek and there were harassed by Indians who shot arrows into three of the oxen. The Indians were not being merely malicious. They had found that the white man destroyed their crops and muddied up their springs and sometimes killed them for no apparent reason. The Indians shot the oxen, hoping to eat the animals when they died.

At Furnace Creek the wagons split, some going northwest, others south. They all found they were caught in a trap between mountains which could not be crossed with wagons. The Jayhawkers burned their wagons and went north, carrying the meat from their slaughtered oxen on their backs. One incredible family, the Wades from England, spanned-up their oxen without a word to anybody and took off southward.

Henry Wade had just turned fifty and with him was his wife Mary, from London, and their four children, Harry, Charles, Almira, and Richard, the oldest fourteen and the youngest five. Theirs was the only wagon that got out of Death Valley, for they found Saratoga Springs and the Mojave River, which appears and disappears, and which led them to Cajon Pass and so to a way out of the valley. The others, not in the Jayhawker party, which had decided to walk out, held a council of war and voted that two of the strongest men should be sent for help on foot. The men selected were William Lewis Manley and John Rogers, the latter from Tennessee. They were expected to be away ten days and were given the best guns and all the money that remained with the party. It amounted to a little over thirty dollars.

Ten days went by, and then fifteen and then twenty. The Bennett family, waiting with the wagons, had three children and there was an infant boy in the Arcane family. Others of the remaining party, despairing of relief, left, so that when three weeks had gone by only four lonely wagons, two deserted, remained in the valley, the children crouching under them all day to keep in the shade.

On the twenty-sixth day, Manley and Rogers came back

with one mule and some supplies. They found a trail of death on their return journey—the grave of one of the Jayhawkers and the unburied body of another. Not far from the wagons they found another body—sun-dried on the floor of Death Valley.

When they came in sight of the wagons, not a soul was to be seen. The tattered canvas tops riffled a little in the hot desert wind, but there was no other movement. "We're too late," said Rogers. "They're likely all dead."

"We'll see," said Manley, and fired a shot into the air. And then there was a slight movement in the shadows under the wagons and a skeleton of a man crawled out and stood up, blinking at them in the terrible sun and unable to say a word. They were all there and they were all alive—even the baby.

Lewis Manley reached into the pack on the mule's back and brought out something. "California gold," he said. "For the children." And he gave them an orange apiece; the gift of a Mexican woman in California who had sent them with her prayers.

Death Valley, surrounded by mountains, has over the centuries become the sump into which minerals washed down by rain have been deposited. It is a mine of them, and it is these which give it the appearance of an inferno—a place which has been visited by consuming flames which left behind only colored ashes. There are spires and ledges and twists and cones of purple and red, of yellow and pink and gray-white formations all about. Out on the salt flats blooms the Devil's Cornfield, a growth of strange arrow-like weeds thrusting up from the bitter soil. And at another place, headed towards the Funeral Mountains on the east side of the valley, you will find a canyon country of sulphurous-looking rocks, carved into peaks and mesas and valleys by the furnace wind.

We journeyed through this landscape in the safety of the bus, but did not get out for it was too hot for sight-seeing on foot. That men should have once worked in this place, mining borax and gypsum and handling hundred-mule teams to take the borax two hundred miles across the mountains and deserts to the nearest railhead, seems incredible. Yet that business went on for years in Death Valley, which must at the time have been the world's center of profanity.

Consider the enormous output of earnest swearing needed to get one hundred mules all headed in the same direction at the same time. I know what I am talking of; for although I have little experience of mules, in my boyhood I handled a cart-horse and am a judge of the profanity required to get any quadruped to work. The cart-horse's name was Blossom and numerous wasps were forever buzzing around her huge feet. She responded only to swearing—real swearing, for the mere pronunciation of the words left her unmoved. The tune was required as well, as Mark Twain once remarked, and only then would Blossom, perpetually lounging against the shaft of the far cart, shift her glossy chestnut hips and move forward. I am one of that generation of men, now dying out, taught to swear by a horse.

I had thought to go up to Scotty's Castle in the north of the valley, where among other out-of-place wonders there is a tremendous organ which operates automatically like a player piano and plays, I believe, "The Last Rose of Summer" with touching dynamics. But the road to Scotty's Castle, through the length of the valley, was closed with a warning that it was impassable, the victim of those tremendous spring rains, which had washed out the approach road through the Panamints. So we turned south, or rather southeast, to the

Visitors Center at Furnace Creek to rest our eyes on the grass of that golf course which nestles in the pit of hell.

The Center we found a stylish modern building of red bricks and plate glass and shaded walks. It belongs to a fashionable shopping district, such as Fifth Avenue, New York, used to be and represents another of those incongruities which abound in Death Valley—the gestures men make to pretend, I think, that they are not frightened. The Center, of course, was closed, for Death Valley is a winter resort visited by a hundred thousand people between November and May and deserted entirely in the summertime. We walked about the fashionable, lonely, deserted building and took Tich, the kitten, with us. She was very hot and, seeing the cool interior of the lounge beckoning, rushed towards it, only to butt her nose against the locked plate-glass door.

A few ants were scurrying over the concrete sidewalks and the ironwood trees shimmered in the sun. There was a thermometer on the wall in the shade and it read 120 degrees. We looked at the grass on the golf course and it had a synthetic look, as if it were of plastic. We looked at the bright bubbling stream flowing by, but the heat was too much. It could not be borne for more than a few minutes and we headed back to the bus, and sighed with relief as we entered. The temperature within was a cool, relaxing 110.

We were in Death Valley, of course, at entirely the wrong time and Hazel, who, as I have said, was born in Arizona and loves the desert, said it would be cool if we headed up into the mountains toward Grand Canyon. I, at the moment, found it hard to believe that it would be cool anywhere on earth, but plainly we must get out of Death Valley to be comfortable.

We moved on out then, passing on our way a monstrous

juggernaut of a steam engine, with vast spiked wheels, by the side of the road. This was a latter-day experiment at replacing the hundred-mule teams in the borax trade with steam power and thus reducing the swearing in Death Valley. This juggernaut of iron—a train which ran without benefit of tracks and, I suppose, a sort of ancestor to the modern tank —hauled the borax cars the same two hundred miles across the mountains and the deserts to the railhead. It must have filled the whole desert with an infernal snorting and clanging and rattling as it clawed and ground its way along. A plaque said the name was "Dinah" and I wondered whether this was the same "Dinah" that somebody was in the kitchen with, playing on the old banjo.

Our road led out to Death Valley Junction on the eastern side of the valley and then on to Lathrop Wells and Las Vegas. It was a long hot road, though considerably cooler when we got to Las Vegas. We did not stop in Las Vegas. I didn't have the nerve. I had the feeling that if I as much as stepped out of the bus I would lose everything I had in a game of poker. There is a kind of frantic air about that city which makes calm thought difficult if not impossible. So we slid down the huge main highway with its monstrous lighted signs advertising food and drink, girls and games and went on to Henderson and then to Boulder.

We went to Boulder because years before—fourteen years before—Hazel and I, driving to New York, had crossed Death Valley in midsummer and become so hot and dried out that our lives had been saved only by reaching the city of Boulder. There we entered an ice cream parlor and luxuriated in vanilla ice cream sodas and glasses of ice water, and Boulder has become for us a paradise on the brink of an inferno. So we headed for Boulder and found the city park and pulled the bus to the side opposite a row of rock elms and tumbled out.

It was wonderful outside. The temperature was but 80 in the shade. We strolled over to the park and lay in the cool grass under the rock elms and listened for a while to the quiet insect sounds. There was also a slight drone which rose from nothing to pianissimo and then died away at regular intervals. It came from way up in the sky where jet plane after jet plane appeared out of the east in the lovely blue heaven and disappeared into the west. Hardly had the contrail of one gone than the contrail of another replaced it. The procession was uninterrupted and the paths of the planes never varied. They followed sky highways as clearly defined as those on land. Sailing to Hawaii, in the middle of the ocean, I have heard that same faint airplane sound and, glancing up, seen the contrail of a jet liner, and a little later another and then another. One could steer by them, I suppose, given clear weather.

Standing by the bus, when we returned after a picnic dinner in the little Boulder park, was a gentleman on crutches. We exchanged a word or two, and since he was interested I showed him through the bus and was emboldened to inquire what had happened to his leg.

"I broke it in a plane crash," he said. The setting sun was touching the tops of the mountains with a splendid light and he pointed with his crutch. "See that notch right next to the snow-capped peak?" he asked. "Me and two other guys. We crashed up there. They were killed. I was lucky. Just a broken leg and some ribs. Right there. Right in that notch. Sometimes I come out here in the evening and look at it. It finished me for flying. They won't give me a license any more. But I got a daughter that likes to fly. She'll maybe fly me around. My wife doesn't fly. Doesn't like it."

Little scraps of his story continued to come from him in this manner—bits about shooting deer (there are many of them in the desert mountains) and flying down, on the spur of a moment, to visit a friend in Salome, Arizona. He wasn't particularly interested in me. He just wanted to talk about himself and the notch in the mountains where he had been saved and his friends had died.

When he had gone I told Kevin about him.

"He ought to make up his mind," said Kevin.

"What do you mean?" I asked.

"He told *me* that he broke his leg stepping into a hole in the road in the dark one night," said Kevin. He had told the same thing to Hazel. On reflection I think the man was a writer. I think he had been standing there on his crutch looking at the range of mountains and the particular notch up on the snowfields and the whole story had come to him in the most vivid details. That is often the way with writers. You look at something and it starts talking to you and all you do really is just put down what it says, whether it is a mountain or a tree or a pool of quiet water.

After dinner it was still too hot to sit in the bus, so we went back to the park for a while. The light was ebbing from the sky and the mountains dissolving into the dark ground. Two bats came stumbling out of the shadows, skittering about in the sky and giving plaintive shrieks.

"What are they?" asked Arabella.

"Bats," I replied.

"Do they suck blood?"

"Yes. Near here there is a huge cave whose mile-long walls are lined with clusters of bats. Towards evening, at about this hour, one or two scouts go out looking for victims. When they find them—perhaps a bearded, bald-headed man and a girl of thirteen with long hair, standing alone in a park, a long way from help—the scouts return to the cave. There is a tremendous rustling of leather wings and a squishing of soft velvet bodies, and out of the cave comes a black swarm of bats seeking their evening banquet."

"I'm not scared," said Arabella.

One of the two bats flung down out of the luminous sky towards my head. "Let's get out of here," I said.

Waiting for the cool of the night to arrive, we took a walk in search of that ice cream parlor which had saved Hazel and me fourteen years before. We found it but it was shut. When the last light had left the sky, the streets were so dark that I walked right through a water sprinkler. On the way back, thinking idly of Samarkand and Persiopolis and the Golden Horde of Genghis Khan, I walked through it again, to the great delight of my children. These are the hazards of the writer, many of whom I suppose, deep in thought, fall off cliffs or down manholes and are killed.

chapter
Five

THE problem of the Grand Canyon is which side to approach it from, for there are of course no bridges across. We chose the north side because we wanted first of all to go to Zion National Park to see again the Great White Throne and the Court of the Patriarchs and all the other tremendous sculpturings of the earth which have exhausted language without ever being described. I see immediately that I pretend that some loftiness of mind drew me to Zion; that the magnificence of those soaring pillars and plinths of brightened earth, with at their tops trees no bigger than match sticks, lured me there to contemplate the insignificance of man and the grandeur of nature.

It was not so.

The fact of the matter is that there is in the bottom of Zion Canyon the biggest and coolest swimming pool I have ever clapped eyes upon. And I was still intolerably hot from Death Valley. No Great White Throne would delight me half as much as diving into that monstrous swimming pool and swimming down to the deepest part of it and lying there luxuriating in coolness and perhaps even coldness until forced to surface for lack of air. Also, the last time we were there, Hazel and I, we had met a girl standing in the fork of the road selling peaches. She was a pretty girl and it was a red road with green growth and the beginning of the canyon walls rising to left and to right. The peaches were twenty-five cents for a dozen. They were delicious. Thinking of how cool and juicy those peaches were and perhaps that the girl was immortal and might still be there (for surely there are in America those beings which exist in Ireland and which solace the stranger on his lonely way), I was in a bit of a hurry to get to Zion for peaches and the swimming pool and maybe a glance at the Great White Throne. And that's the truth of the matter.

First, however, I had to buy a belt to hold up my pants. I have reached the age in life when there is an increase in my waist line and it is my contention that this was provided by the Almighty to caution me against bending over too much. Hazel thinks differently and sent me off to buy a belt which would both keep up my pants and hold in my corporation. She sent Kevin and Christopher with me because I am not a very good shopper. The reason for that is that I "buy for shiny." Show me anything that is all clean and spangly and shiny and I'm likely to buy it. That's the way I buy fishing rods and automobiles and dishwashers and refrigerators and so on. It is the secret of American financial strength for it lies at the bottom of all American merchandising. Polish whatever you have to sell and you will find a customer, for people are children and do not buy the thing itself but the shininess of the thing.

All that was involved at present, however, was a belt and it was quite ridiculous of Hazel to send Kevin and Christopher with me to see that I didn't get taken. We found a lovely cool store full of knicknacks. I can't remember a single one of them, but they gave me the same thrill that going to Woolworth's around Christmas time used to give me when I was a child. There was a stockwhip of braided leather. I remember that and was looking at it closely when Kevin reminded me I was supposed to be buying a belt. There was some really nice clean-looking stationery with a road runner, in color, printed on it. I bought some of that meaning to use it to answer letters, at which I am not very good. There were also some string ties—Western style. They are made of strips of leather and have a big piece of Indian jewelry on them. I was looking them over when Kevin mentioned belts again. So I found the belts and to get the whole thing over with gave one to the lady running the shop and said that would suit me.

"See if it will fit you, Dad," said Kevin.

It didn't. I found one that did and paid for it and when I got out Kevin said, "Dad, did you have to buy the most expensive belt in the store?"

"That wasn't the most expensive belt in the store," I said.

"It sure was," said Kevin. "It's hand-tooled leather. Cost six dollars. You could have got one for a buck fifty." Which caused me to wonder what I used to do when I went shopping before Kevin was around.

Ours was never a family to start early in the morning. There are too many of us and none of us likes to be hustled. It was ten o'clock before we got started. In late June it is very hot in Boulder City at ten in the morning. We turned on the air conditioners and one of them—the big one operated by that outside generator with its little separate gasoline engine—broke down immediately.

"We have become one with the heat," Kevin wrote in the log and so we had. With only the forward and smaller air-conditioning unit operating, the interior temperature in the bus was 100 degrees. Tich, the kitten, took a saucer of milk, licked a piece of ice and disappeared behind the back of the sofa. The heat became intolerable and we decided to rely on the wind to cool us and turned off the air conditioning unit and opened all the windows and air vents. This left the thermometer at a hundred degrees but produced an impression of coolness because of the air flow. I gave the wheel to Kevin, Christopher took over in the pilot seat, Hazel went into the main cabin to die in solitude and I sat with Patricia, Rory, Cormac and Arabella in the dinette area and had them teach me gin rummy again.

I have a very good memory for all kinds of odd things but none at all for cards. Sitting at this typewriter right now I can remember the definition of a logarithm, the first four bars of the viola score of the "Eroica," at least ten lines of the king's speech before the storming of Harfleur in *Henry V*, the date of the last battle fought on English soil (Sedgemoor, 1685) and the first name of Pontius Pilate's wife (it was Procula), but though I have played hundreds of hands, I can't begin to tell you anything about the rules for playing gin rummy.

Coco explained them to me, his little freckled face animated with excitement. His brother, Rory, acted as censor and corrected him about every half sentence. The explanation went like this, "You've got to get all threes . . ."

". . . or four of anything."

"Or you can have four of them."

"Of what? Fours or threes? I mean four fours but three threes?"

"No. Four of anything. Even kings."

"And then you can have a run—like two, three, four, and so on."

"How many?"

"All the cards in your hand."

"Who wins?"

"The guy that gets out first. Like if I had four fours and three fives and I threw away a king . . ."

"It doesn't have to be a king. You can throw away anything."

"Could you throw away one of the fours?"

"Gosh, Dad. What would you want to throw away the four for? You're collecting fours."

"Okay. Let's start."

"Who wants some Kool-Aid?" This from Patricia.

The whole universe wanted Kool-Aid. Arabella even got Tich from behind the sofa and gave her some. Then we started to play. I lost again. I always lose because I like kings and queens and don't care for threes and fours. Tricia explained that you are not supposed to play it that way. You're not supposed to collect the cards that you like but just the cards that other people seem to be throwing away. Cormac won and then Rory won and then Cormac won again. And it seemed to me that I would do much better trying to play "The Fox" on the guitar.

I can sing "The Fox" pretty well and everybody in my family loves it. I learned it years ago from Ed Meagher when we took a drive together up to Tacoma, Washington. But I never learned to play it on the guitar, which is an instrument that can be played by only a certain class of people. It isn't at all true that anyone can learn to play the guitar. That is a common fallacy. I can't learn to play the guitar for one. I can't get my fingers to play the slightest attention to my voice. My fingers don't like my voice and they always come in before or after they are supposed to and make my voice so nervous that I can't sing. But I had a go at "The Fox" on the guitar and failed again and so took out my viola.

I do much better on the viola. I played "The Fox," and "The Rakes of Mallow" and a fair rendering of Dvorak's "Humoreske," and was starting on "The Last Rose of Summer" when Kevin wheeled the bus into a roadside gas station and flung open the door. The filling station attendant stuck his head through it and there was I with a viola and Patricia trying out the guitar and Arabella feeding a piece of ice to the kitten on the table.

"You folks from Los Angeles?" the man asked. I agreed that we were and that seemed to soothe him.

We got thirty gallons of gasoline and took on a little water. The attendant treated us with silent caution. I decided to try to fix the generator engine and pulled the bus to the side and started work. I disconnected the gas line to the tiny carburetor and sucked on it and got gasoline—raw burning gas, so there was no air lock on that side. I took off the filter and found it unblocked. I thought about fiddling with the carburetor but decided against that though I did check that gasoline was coming through the delivery side to the engine.

The service station man watched all this with increasing interest. "Know something about engines?" he asked.

"Only how they work," I replied. "I'm not much at adjusting them."

"What's the matter with it?"

"Stalls out—probably not getting fuel."

"Might be ignition," he offered.

"Might be. But I think it's a fuel pump."

"Say, mister. Mind me asking what was that you were playing when you came here?"

"A viola—it's a kind of man-sized violin."

I showed it to him and was no longer a nut from Los Angeles. I said we were going up to Zion and the Grand Canyon.

"That rig must cost you a lot of money," he ventured.

I explained that I was chartering it and mentioned the charter price. He gave a low whistle.

"It's expensive all right," I said. "But there's eight of us and we're all having a vacation together. We can cook our own meals and we don't have to pay for a motel room at night. In motels in midsummer it would cost a lot of money for eight people. And then we'd have to eat in restaurants. My sons are growing up. This may be the last time we can have a vacation together as a family."

"I got a family myself," he said. "They sure grow up fast."

It was a commonplace saying. It is what all parents say to each other. But it made brothers of us immediately, for children do grow up awfully fast. Eighteen or twenty years is all you have from infancy to departure, and that's a very short time. And then must come a sort of emptiness; a huge house with practically nobody in it and memories in every room.

I couldn't fix the generator. The thing would start, run for a while, and then stop. The heat was appalling. I quit working on the generator and we drove on towards Zion and that enormous ocean-sized, huge swimming pool.

The pretty girl with the peaches had gone, however. I recalled the exact spot in the road and looked for her and she was not there. But a little farther on there was a fruit stand operated by some children and here we bought not only peaches but cherries and nectarines and grapes. They were delicious. Have you ever noticed that fresh fruit is never hot? You can stand a peach in the sun for hours and yet when you eat it, it will be cool.

We luxuriated in the fruit and I refrained from asking the children whether their mother was a witch with long auburn hair who years before had sold peaches in the road a little farther away. I think they were her children. There was a little girl with the same shade of hair and dark and mischievous gray eyes. And the peaches tasted exactly the same, and no one else on earth has such peaches. They come, I think, from Eden and grow in a little grove about a hundred yards southwest of where the tree with the forbidden fruit stands.

At last we entered Zion along the road that travels up the canyon floor, through the cool shade of the trees, with the merriment of water nearby and a soft wind stirring the leaves of the sycamores. It was wonderful to get out of the glare and the blinding heat, not to have to squint your eyes, but to open them wide and see soft shadows and cool grasses and hear the pipe and twitter of birds.

"Will there be bears?" asked Coco. He adores bears.

"No. But there may be deer," I said, and on we went, impatiently pushing towards the vast swimming pool with its crystal-blue water reflecting the azure of God's sky overhead.

But when we got to the pool, something had happened to it. It wasn't huge any more. It was quite small. You couldn't launch yourself from one side and swim for half an hour to the other. You could almost swim across it underwater. Was it only memory that had enlarged it so—made it seem vast and at least lake-sized? Or had the Department of the Interior reduced the size? I think the fault lay with the Interior Department.

The swimming pool seemed to me to be in a different place. It was definitely smaller. But at least it was full of water, and after the first twinge of disappointment we all changed into swimsuits and plunged in. Kevin made it first, and then Christopher and I hard on his heels. I took a mighty leap and dived in and very nearly died. For that water was snow-field cold. It was cold enough to hurt and when I surfaced I swam with haste to the side and got out, pausing only to assure Hazel that it was beautiful. I was not believed, however, and Hazel entered by her own excruciating method—inch by inch down a ladder.

It was enormous fun though. I don't think there is a swimming pool in the world as lovely as this one in the bottom of Zion Canyon. You may lie on your back in the water looking up at the cobalt sky and at the sides of the canyon, red as glowing coals, and the crisp green of the conifers which take root in every possible ledge. This is millionaire living and I think the cost was about a dollar a person. My younger boys, Rory and Cormac, leaped a thousand times off the diving board into that lovely cold water, piping like birds, and were joined in this fun by Kevin, Christopher and Arabella. But Patricia, after a while, was lost in the dreamland of eighteen years of age.

And so the golden afternoon slipped by and the sun dipped behind the canyon rim, a cold shadow not quite matching the temperature of the water flowed over the canyon bottom, and I issued my standard stern orders to my family to get out of the pool and get dressed. When this had been accomplished I got back into the pool myself, for the heavy burden of fatherhood should surely carry with it a few perks. (I wasn't really using my head here—the towels were all damp when I came to need them.)

Then I made a round of the trailer parks in Zion. All were

full, of course, for the procedure is to call ahead and make reservations. All full that is, but one, pleasantly situated by the side of the river and without a single occupant. But this, a park ranger told me, a trifle embarrassed, was reserved for "organized groups." I glanced about the bus. Everybody had their hair combed and looked clean and tidy. "We are a very well-organized group," I said. "There are eight of us and our organization is called a family. It is one of the oldest organizations in the world."

But it wasn't the kind of organization for which that area of the park was reserved. The ranger smiled and said he couldn't let us stay there. He suggested a camp outside the park, and we went there (perhaps not to the one he had in mind) and it was not very attractive. So I decided we would not stay in Zion, but would give it a quick look through and go on towards Grand Canyon.

But let me pause for a moment and compliment the Interior Department on Zion and the other National Parks we visited. They were splendidly kept and the personnel always courteous, and I think the nation would do well to recruit its diplomats from the staff of the National Park Service.

Headed then out of Zion and cool for the first time in days, we drove up the canyon, using a map provided by the Interior Department, and stopped at a viewpoint from which could be seen the Court of the Patriarchs. We dismounted and climbed a little hill to the viewpoint and, solemn as Biblical figures, the tremendous columns or plinths or mesas which constitute the Court of the Patriarchs lay before us. There are several of them, each representing a figure, and they seemed, with bowed heads, to be gathered in silent meditation on some tremendous truth. At this point the canyon is wider and the sun had not gone beyond its western rim. The eastern walls glowed and then in a moment darkened like the quenching of a hot coal and a flurry of wind and rain scoured down on us.

"Look," said Arabella.

We looked and there, stock still, was a deer, more still than a statue and that because it had the ability to move. It was a moment of magic, this encounter between deer and children. They looked at each other in wonder, but without fear, as if they had in a twinkle been moved into each other's dimension. So Heaven must seem when we find it—a place we knew was there and yet wonderful that it should be there. Ears cocked, eyes luminous and soft, the deer took a dainty step towards the children, sniffing the air, and then turned and vanished. We went back into the bus silent and entranced.

We drove out of Zion along a snaking road that climbed the walls of the canyon. We drove not merely through space but through time, through Pleistocene and Oligocene and Miocene and other ages and I rummaged around in my mind for bits of geology, trying to identify sandstones and formations and epochs. Fragments of information came my way—Chinle formation, Navajo sandstone (or is it limestone?), Sundance Sea. My lecture was no model of how to interest children in the wonders of the earth.

"The red stuff," I said, "is Navajo sandstone. It's the ground-down remains of mountain ranges that existed millions of years ago miles away from this place. This was all a flat valley or basin and the sandstone was washed down from the mountains and collected here. It's several hundred feet thick as you can see, so you can imagine how vast the mountains were from which it came."

"When are we going to have dinner?" asked Rory.

I am used to that and so continued. "That white stuff on the top is Kaibab limestone," I said. "It is marine in origin. There was a sea here once called the Sundance Sea and that Kaibab formation was laid down at that time."

"There's a sandwich in the brown paper sack," said Hazel.

"You can find marine fossil—shells and so on and even shark's teeth—in the Kaibab formation," I said.

"There's two sandwiches," said Rory.

I gave up and settled the more immediate problem of dividing two sandwiches among six people. Hazel and Patricia didn't want any.

There is a mile-long tunnel leading out of Zion Canyon. It is the practice in my family for everyone to hold his breath when we go through a tunnel, but this one defeated us. The tunnel was far too long. But the tunnel was one of the highlights of the visit to Zion, because the view through the ports is spectacular, and also because in the evening I had started reading Tolkien's *The Hobbit* to the children. So a rumor was spread that the tunnel had been made by dwarfs looking for treasure in the mountains and there was maybe a dragon at the other end of it by the name of Smaug. Also, when I stopped the bus in mid-tunnel in a dark place, Coco said he could hear marching feet behind us, as if dwarfs were approaching. This, however, proved to be a camper with valve trouble.

It was still light when we left the tunnel for leaving the canyon bottom we had soared from night into day. Around was an amazing plateau of the Chinle sandstone which looked like soft mounds of peach-colored ice cream through which someone had drawn a comb, first one way and then another, leaving numerous parallel lines running through it. These sandstones were laid down in the Permian Period, which was a time of dryness rather like the present, when deserts were extensive over the face of the earth. The wind caused the combed effect, blowing the sand first one way and then another—crossbedding is the geologist's term. Using radioactive dating and a compass, one could perhaps work out the direction of prevailing winds in this region of the world two hundred and fifty million years ago when Earth was a vast reptile farm and before the first Theriodonts or "beast-toothed" reptiles, from whom all mammals descend, appeared.

I explained all this to the children (or as much as I could remember, which wasn't a great deal) and they received it with politeness. I said a few wise words about cotylosaurs or "stem" reptiles and their importance as the ancestors of just about everything on earth.

The children said nothing for they were thinking of dinner. I began to think of dinner myself for breakfast in the heat of Boulder had been sketchy and we had had only sandwiches for lunch. A steak, I thought, would be heavenly.

The steak was a long way off, however. We drove and drove and drove, or so it seemed, as the light was leached from the sky. At last we slipped down the broad sweep of a dark hill and found at the foot of it one of those magnificent motel-gas-station-restaurant combinations with which American enterprise is, thank God, lousing up the wilderness.

In this oasis we did not have steak, but we had roast beef and salad and potatoes and pie and coffee. And then, cool at last and full, we went back to the bus for a good night's sleep.

chapter

Six

WE HAD parked the bus for the night in a small trailer camp facing a river and just off State Highway 15. There were a number of other trailers parked alongside of us, and these were for the greater part owned by people who were not merely taking a holiday in a mobile home, but lived in trailers all year long. Most drove real trailers—that is to say trailers pulled by cars, one advantage being that you can unhitch the trailer at a park and then drive the car into town for stores.

Two middle-aged ladies, plump, gray-haired and competent, were in the trailer to port—a huge trailer far bigger than our bus. They hitched it up to their car very competently indeed, making our efforts at assistance quite unneeded, though they courteously endured them. They asked us about going through the tunnel in Zion—whether we had had any difficulty at corners. We had not, because the bus had such a short wheel base. But they, with the long trailer, did not dare attempt the tunnel lest they get stuck at a corner. They had to take some devious route into Zion Canyon.

These two, past their prime and alone, were our first introduction to trailer people—a segment of the American public, growing rapidly, which moves about the United States from border to border, following routes dictated by the weather and perhaps sufficiently defined to be called migration routes. Most we met were retired, their families grown. They had a great awareness of weather and of vegetation and of animal life. They had lived one life in raising their families and following their trades or professions, and they were now engaged in living another life, and perhaps this second life of wandering about, looking at the country in which they were born, learning its size, its variety and its history, would complete the first life when so much time had to be spent in the drudgery of earning a living.

The trailer people have solved the retirement problem beautifully, for they are not just kept active to make the time pass, but are enjoying and fully using their time. They are a product of the reforms of the thirties, which brought in social security and pension plans and other forms of income for those not working. Their own parents, retired, probably had to stay at home for lack of money to go anywhere. Not so today and perhaps these adventurous senior citizens will have a growing effect on the nation's government, for they have time to think and much of their thinking is in the area of preserving the natural resources of the country—clean air and clean water among them. There will be more and more of them, and they will exert a bigger and bigger political influence and all to the good, I believe. Certainly they have already brought into being a new industry—manufacturing trailers and campers, and the way in which the smallest areas in these trailers are put to use is admirable.

The two ladies left before we even had coffee going, backing their vast trailer competently out of the parking lot and then pulling into the highway. On the other side of us a neat man who had spent his life in the Customs Service hitched up his trailer alone. To do this he had to back the car inch by inch to the place where he thought the trailer hitch was. Kevin and I gave him a few directions, but he said he was quite accustomed to doing this himself, having over the years developed the knack of feeling, as it were, where the trailer hitch was, several feet from the driver's seat which he occupied backing up. His family was grown, he said, and he and his wife had been roaming the country for several years.

"You get an itch to travel," he said shyly, "when you work in the Customs Service."

Soon we were the only occupants of the trailer court, for we did not follow that rule of early departure of the trailer people. We had a leisurely breakfast, gassed up the bus (it took a monstrous thirty and forty gallons of gasoline at a gulp each day, but thank goodness, consumed regular gasoline and not ethyl) and then pulled out onto U.S. Highway 89A towards the north rim of the Grand Canyon.

The approach to the Grand Canyon on this route is an ascent, the road first crossing a vast desert area, flat and thickly covered with sagebrush. There are, or should be, mountains on the horizon—the Kaibabs—but I could not see them. Then, right in the middle of this desert, where nothing grew higher than two feet and it seemed there could not be a tree for hundreds of miles, there was a lumber mill. No mistake about it. There it was, and we could hear the whine of the saws and see the great logs stacked up ready for cutting. But where did they come from?

Well, they came from the forests in the sky as we discovered on seeing a little plume of dust rolling across the desert towards us. This turned out to be a lumber truck, carrying big logs of fir and pine from the Kaibab National Forest hundreds of feet above our heads and many, many miles to the east. This is one of the topsy turvy conditions of the American Southwest. The low areas are all dry and desert, and the high mountaintops are cool and verdant, holding hidden valleys and icy streams. This is a contradiction of topography in other parts—in the Eastern states, for instance. There, the low valleys are lush and contain the meadows. The mountaintops may be forested, but the higher they go, the more stark and denuded of growth until finally, on the peaks, you meet desert.

I first came across this upside-down condition in Baja California, when I set out with a friend to ascend by truck a mountain range known as San Pedro Mártir. In this range there are peaks of ten thousand feet or more, and between them lovely valleys forested, shaded, growing ferns, it is said, and with deer abounding and trout in the streams. But at the foot of these mountains there is searing hot desert—desert so torrid and so dry that it is foolishness in midsummer to get out of your truck or car. Paradise in the sky then, and the Inferno below. Did this condition, I wonder, common to many desert countries, give rise to our concept of Heaven above and Hell below? For we got that concept from the Hebrews, and perhaps the same condition existed in their country. Perhaps there were hot, waterless deserts at sea level, and parklands with shade and plenty to drink, in the higher mountain folds.

There is really no reason otherwise why we should think of Heaven being above, and when we leave Earth, of course, there isn't any above or below. But then, Heaven is not a direction but a dimension; not a location but a condition, and the reason the Soviet cosmonauts who first circled Earth in a sputnik did not see any angels was because you cannot see an angel any more than you can see an idea. Nonetheless ideas do exist and angels as well, I believe. It is amusing to note how those who dismiss angels carry a rabbit foot, or consult their horoscope in the daily paper.

We crossed the floor of Hell, then, and started to mount slowly into Paradise, and as we did so, the vegetation changed subtly. For a long time there was nothing to see but the sage-brush. Then came other desert plants—creosote bush with its tiny dark-green leaves and spindly branches. It burns with a lovely hot bright flame, but is soon consumed. Then piñons—the tiny dwarfed pines which produced a nut once an important source of food among Indians. A few hundred feet higher and we were among twenty-foot pines and firs and then, without any dramatic change, among ponderosa pines growing amid clumps of firs and thickets of silver birch with their lovely pale-green leaves.

The road now traveled through cool summer meadows of enormous length. These meadows were perhaps half a mile across, and were bordered with forest of pine and birch, and there was an impression of immensity about them which was very consoling.

We drove happily down that long road in Paradise, known to the mapmakers as the Kaibab National Forest. We stopped the bus, in which the temperature had now declined to an astonishing 70 degrees, and we walked over the sun-drenched meadow, flanked by firs and birches, which seemed to slide to the horizon and then on to eternity. The wind was cool, almost crisp and it made a lovely hiss over the short, stiff grass.

The grass, closely examined, was really a flower bed, for there were tiny carmine dots of scarlet pimpernel here and there, and lovely delicate harebells of palest blue. I had been a long time in the city and I had forgotten the sounds of the countryside. They seeped back to me now—the wind sounds and bird sounds and even the crunch of my boots on little ridges of stiff clay and the tinkling of stones as we walked along a graveled path.

I found I had forgotten, since boyhood, what it is like to walk over ground which has not been leveled to a pavement flatness. I stumbled several times before I recovered the knack of letting my feet be loose at the ankle so that they could immediately accommodate to whatever gradient they met. Many of the flowers about I knew, such as larkspur and fringed gentian, but many were strange and I had not at the time a book in which to identify them.

It would have been delightful to have camped in some corner of one of these vast meadows, but signs forbade camping. We went back to the bus and journeyed on a little and came to the La Motte Camping Ground and, on the road leading to it, a hitching rail where horses could be had for riding.

All the children wanted to ride, which meant six horses, that being, thank God, the available supply, so I was not required to go with them. I have ridden horses several times but am of a generation which was never comfortable on a horse. Modern children, because of television, have no fear of horses. They see so much of horses that they look upon them as friendly, kind, considerate creatures on the side of law and order. I know different. You will recall that I was taught to swear by a horse. I was also taught never to pass round the rear of a horse or he would likely, in a kind, considerate, companion-like manner kick your backbone out. Horses, discovered in my childhood, like to stand on your feet when you are dismounted holding the reins. And some of them, every now and then, will bite you out of pure love—or because they think you are an apple.

My approach to horses then differs from that of my children. I know that good old Trigger has probably tossed Roy Rogers into the next county several times, but my kids don't know that. They all wanted to ride horses, and after taking solemn farewell of them and commending them for their courage (which I assured them matched my own when young), I hired six horses and off they went.

Nothing happened to them. Maybe, since my time, horses have been watching television too. They behaved perfectly. They didn't shy, buck, bite, kick, fight each other and head for the nearest low branch on which to dislodge their riders. They posed for pictures which I took. Then Kevin's horse passed gracefully by me, tried to stand on my foot, and they all trotted up the meadow and behind a clump of silver birch and Hazel and I went back to the bus to fix lunch—peanut butter sandwiches for the children, should they survive, and meat sandwiches for me, for I cannot abide peanut butter, which I know to be chemically indestructible. (Once while sailing to Catalina Island, I threw a peanut butter sandwich—kindly provided by my host—overboard and it followed us at five and a half knots over to Catalina thirty miles away, where it bobbed about in the wake of the ship for two days. We managed to give it the slip in the dark on the third night.)

The May family from Nevada rented the horses—two boys of high-school age and a little girl, who had caught a chipmunk which she had in a glass bottle with holes punched in the top for air.

"He's a nice little fellow," I said.

"You can have him for a dollar," she replied prettily. She was a lovely little creature, chubby and strong and freckled and, I think, with auburn hair cut in a bob. Her brothers, with Western hats of felt and chaps over their jeans, were entirely competent with horses. They didn't wear those jeans for show. They were working horsemen or cowboys, with a rare, sly sense of humor, and a great deal of patience. They owned a pet raven which had flown off and was amusing people in a neighboring trailer camp. It was a remarkable bird, very large, and although it could not say "nevermore" or anything that I could understand, it had a great fondness for the stones which children were feeding to it. It took each stone with delight in its strong white beak and chomped on it a little, ruminating on the likely taste, and then dropped it for another.

The boys and their sister were handling the horses for their father, who was a schoolteacher in Nevada and would be up the following day. They asked Kevin not to run his horse, as it had only just arrived from the lowlands, and was unaccustomed to the heights.

"If you gallop him it will kill him," they said.

Kevin promised to take it easy. One of the May brothers went off with my children to see them safe since they were not accustomed to riding horses. They were nice people, considerate, competent, good-humored and easygoing. The country could do with about a million more of them.

chapter *Seven*

THERE is no apt phrase with which to sum up the Grand Canyon. All the words dealing with size and with majesty have been so much used on meaner things that they are inadequate to describe this massive, jagged wound in the flesh of earth.

Deep down the wound goes, driving towards the vitals; towards that last shield of rock which divides our cool and pleasant surface from the primordial things below. It plunges into the pit of the world, and through the earth's history to cryptozoic time—the time of "secret life" six hundred million years ago. It is a place to be looked at in silence and awe, there being no adequate description of it.

I had had a plan about the Grand Canyon—a wonderful adventure to be undertaken by the whole family. It was to ride down to the bottom of it on mules along Bright Angel Trail and then out again. I thought what fun it would be to go down through the ages of the world from the Cenozoic and the Mezosoic and into the Paleozoic, past the bones of the monsters that had their time on earth, the "Terrible Lizards" and the "Toothed Birds" and the "Maze Toothed Things," and deep down to the creatures having no teeth and no skeleton but living in vast shells, creatures such as the ammonite and the nautilus and down even further to the trilobites and the algae and the primitive worms whose fragile burrows, five hundred million years old, have out-endured a thousand times all the works of man.

However, when we had parked the bus near Bright Angel Point and walked from the parking lot down a little trail to suddenly find the whole earth falling away from us, nobody wanted to take a burro ride down into the canyon. It seemed indeed that if you did not back away from the edge of that void, some power would suck you over and down to the bottom where, peeping between the trees over the ledges of precipices, themselves several hundred feet below, you could catch a glimpse of the thread of the river in the canyon bottom.

It is the river that made the Grand Canyon. The mountain range that first brought the river into being is gone to dust millions of years ago, replaced by another and then another and then another. But the river remained, and as the earth started to rise in its way, the river cut through as a circular saw will cut through a log rolled towards its teeth. The higher the earth rose, the deeper the river cut, sawing through the strata or growth rings of Earth until it has now sawed through into the Precambrian core.

The expedition to the bottom of the canyon then was ruled out by the view from the top, and further condemned by the fact that it would take two or three days to accomplish. We contented ourselves with trembling on the rim, hearing the buffeting of the wind as it rolled over the canyon top and met the currents of hot air rising from the depths. Ravens whirled about in this vortex of air like black rags, above the ragged pines and firs, some split by lightning or tumbled over by the winter winds.

We did, however, go down a foot-trail at Bright Angel Point from the monstrous lodge of gray stone on the canyon rim which I think is occupied, at a certain time of the year, by giants and anthropophagi. It is no more intended for humans than the canyon itself.

The foot-trail led by seductively easy stages to a lookout position at Bright Angel Point where, buffeted by the monstrous torrent of wind, we clung to an iron railing and looked straight down the canyon at its scalded mounds and stratified sides and match-sized conifers growing, some out of red, and others out of white and gray, clays and sandstones.

The Grand Canyon is one of those places which have to be seen to be disbelieved. It is too big, too complicated for storytelling. You must look and be numbed, and get comfort from seeing little chipmunks and ground squirrels here and there, nibbling on nuts and seeds. I have never felt friendlier to squirrels than when we both clung to the sides of the Grand Canyon and they with their quick movements and bright eyes did their best to calm me. Their ease reduced my disquiet. I went out on a ledge which was six foot thick at least, to take a picture, and had to lean against the wind to get the right angle. If it had let up for a moment, I suppose, I would have fallen over—and Arabella too, for she was holding on to my belt to prevent accident.

Then came the road back up to the rim, which I was surprised to find on turning to face it was now several hundred feet above our heads; up wearying flights of stairs which I had hardly noticed in descending. Some years ago (I think about fifteen years ago or perhaps a trifle longer) I was placed under a spell by some creatures whom I unwittingly offended. The result was that I, a boy, was clothed in the flesh of an aging man. My skin lost much of its elasticity. My hair dissolved from the top of my head. My beard showed gray. My eyes saw things less sharply and my heart and lungs found work in what was previously play. This happened subtly as is the way with spells and so, though a boy in my interior, I walk around weighed down by the increasing handicaps of age and until I can find the counter-spell, matters are going to get worse rather than better for me.

My children understand this affliction and sympathize to that degree which is possible with children. Seeing that I could not run to the top with them, off they went, and I toiled upwards with Hazel (who has been subject to a like spell), surprised that there should be more steps on the way up than there were on the way down.

But I found a fossil. There it was jutting out of the Toroweap formation, the fossilized shell of some kind of gastropod, two hundred million years old glinting in the limestone in the twentieth-century sun. I then performed a miracle. I reached out and touched it. Not a miracle, you say? Oh yes, it certainly was. The mathematical chances that I, Leonard Wibberley, born in Dublin, Ireland, April 9, 1915, should find this particular gastropod, of all the billions of gastropods contemporary with it, are beyond calculation. How much further than beyond calculation was the chance that I, having miraculously come upon this miraculously preserved gastropod, should decide to touch it? Astronomical indeed and beyond astronomical.

No, it was a miracle and I performed it with reverence and deliberation. This live thing that is myself reached out and touched that thing that was once alive and a bond was formed between us; an intimacy which stretched across two hundred million years. I went on consoled. A little farther on a ground squirrel threw me a seed. You may think he merely dropped it and it rolled in my direction. But I think he really threw it to me for between me and the ground squirrel and the gastropod was that mystic link which we call life.

When we at last got to the top, out of breath, buffeted by the Grand Canyon wind, we had hamburgers in the giant's house, made perhaps in the kitchen where, as I explained to the children, at other times bread is baked of the bones of Englishmen to a roaring chorus of "Fee, fie, foe, fum." Then everybody wanted to buy souvenirs and I had to admit that however glaring, brash, vulgar, tinselly and tawdry souvenir shops are—and many are all of those things—I am very fond of them.

Coco wanted a stockwhip of braided leather, and when I had told him three times that he could not have it, for he would undoubtedly cut his brother Rory in half with it, I bought it for him anyway and his joy was worth the price many times over. His brother, I decided, would have to look after himself. Kevin bought a miniature beaded Indian belt to hang in his bus and the girls bought pieces of jewelry. Hazel bought postcards and some dolls, I think, and Christopher a ring of Indian silver. I got a collection of small stones and minerals in a box, all identified by unpronounceable names, and some more stationery with which to answer the letters that I never answer. Then we boarded the bus once more, and headed back to the La Motte camping ground, where we had decided to stay for the night so the children could have another ride on those fine horses the next day.

There was, of course, no place to camp—the sites being occupied. But we found a little copse of fir and silver birch off the road, where there was another camper already in position, and we pulled in here. It was a lovely place to camp and not more than a quarter of a mile stroll to the washrooms at the campsite proper. A tiny birch tree, five feet high, grew a few feet away from the site of the bus—a perfectly proportioned and enchanting miniature of a full-grown tree. A boy came along and murdered it. He grabbed it by the top, twisted it, and with a knife which he had bought for use in the outdoors, sawed through its tiny trunk. Having done that, he flung the little tree on the ground and went off, and in half an hour the leaves were withering. No one, I suppose, had ever taught him that great Commandment, "Thou shalt not kill."

Despite the slaughter of the little tree, we had a lovely night of it in that copse of fir and pines in the high mountain meadow of the Kaibab National Forest. We read a chapter from *The Hobbit* after dinner—the one where the wise and lordly eagles rescue the Hobbit and the dwarfs from the terrible Wargs. Then Hazel carefully explained to everybody how to play contract bridge and we played cards, amid more laughter than is permitted at bridge. Then it was time to get down the beds, say prayers and lie in the tremendous darkness with the trees and the grass, listening to the questing wind, until we fell asleep.

chapter
Eight

THE following morning I decided once again to fix the auxiliary generator—the little gasoline engine which operated the air-conditioning unit and helped to keep the batteries supplying interior lighting to the bus fully charged. I will say immediately that the only thing I did right in trying to fix it was to have breakfast first.

Kevin and Christopher took Patricia, Arabella, Rory, and Cormac down to the Mays' hitching rail to talk to them and to ride the horses again, and I got out my kit of tools and tackled the generator. The thing, as I have explained, would start, run for a little while and then stop. Plainly the trouble was not electrical. It seemed that there was an interruption of the fuel supply. The fuel came from the main tanks of the bus, so there was no question of the tank having run dry.

I undid the fuel line with a prayer to that particular sprite who is in charge of stripping the threads on brass nuts to look the other way. Not a drop of gasoline came out of it. Cautiously I bent the copper pipe to a position in which I could suck on it, and sucked. I got air. Not fresh air, of course, but air heavily laced with the fumes of Texaco 80-plus octane gasoline—a rich, full, acrid and brassy flavor which immediately numbed the softer membrane of my mouth and nostrils.

The fact that I was getting fumes and not liquid gasoline meant, of course, an air lock—a bubble or a column of air in the line which broke the vacuum feeding to the carburetor. (I had checked the line and found that there was no pump, the feed to the carburetor being dependent on the siphon principle. You know the siphon principle, of course. It says roughly that you can transfer a liquid from a higher to a lower level through a tube if you first suck all the air out of the tube and then have the good luck not to allow any more to get back into it. I never had much luck with siphons. I fixed one for Arabella recently for her school physics class and the fact that I could fix it at all astonished her more than the principle on which it worked.)

I was not so fortunate with the gasoline fuel line on the generator. I sucked huge quantities of gasoline fumes out of it, blocking off the reentry of air with my tongue and eventually was rewarded with a huge cold gulp of pure Texaco which numbed the end of my tongue, swelled my lips to the size of frankfurters, and detached my nose so that it seemed to be floating four inches in front of my face and anxious to go further. But I'm hardy. I've fixed gasoline engines hanging upside down on a yacht in a quartering sea.

I spat out the mouthful of gasoline, and with blurry eyes managed to get the fuel line to the carburetor and hook it up. Then I pressed the starter. The engine fired immediately. I sat triumphant on the grass, mopping my tongue with my sleeve, staring at God's blue sky with watery eyes and rejoicing that man should be the master of the machinery he invented. I was wrong. The engine stopped. I went through the whole process again. In fact, I did it so many times that, believe it or not (and it is hard to believe), I got to the point where I didn't particularly mind getting a mouthful of cold gasoline. But the engine each time started, ran for but a few seconds, and then stopped.

So I took the carburetor off, and examined the filters and cleaned out the bowl, and held it upside down and blew through it, and there wasn't anything wrong with the carburetor that I could find. Once a fuel problem gets beyond a carburetor, I'm licked. I put the whole contrivance back together again and concentrated on trying to get my nose to rejoin my face and my tongue not to reject my lips as strangers.

A tall, elderly man, using a stout hazel stick with which to walk, came over to me from a nearby trailer. He looked at me with patience out of eyes the color of harebells, and leaned a little on his stick, which he had before him. "Trouble?" he asked, and I explained the difficulty.

I went through my whole theory of what was the matter and what I had done to remedy it, and he listened with interest but said nothing. He was very wise. When a man has been frustrated in his attempt to make a piece of machinery work, it is much better to let him believe that there is a spirit of malevolence in that particular piece of machinery than to offer him a logical explanation of his failure. So the tall and noble-looking man said nothing, but looked about him at the length of that mountain meadow—it was well over three miles long at that place and I would say a good half-mile from side to side where it was bordered by the trees. His eyes moved on to the horizons and in that patient gaze he gave me to understand that the generator did not matter. I gathered up my tools gratefully.

"I see you're from California," he said.

"I am," I replied, and explained where we had been and how we had got the bus. And then I asked him for advice, for he was plainly an expert in the matter of trailer living.

"Is it all right to camp by the side of the road if you can't find a proper camping site?" I asked, for this business of finding a camping site concerned me, particularly since in the National Parks there were notices forbidding camping outside specified areas.

He considered the question for a while and to help with his consideration, he poked at a little twig on the ground with the end of his stick. "Yes," he said. "It is all right to do that. But you've got to beware of thugs. There are a lot of them around—traveling the roads—and campers are an easy mark for them.

"Just a little while back I heard of a young couple in a trailer who camped by the side of the road and went to sleep with the door unlocked. Well, while they were asleep, somebody got into their trailer and robbed them of every penny they had. They hadn't hidden their money, of course. It was in the man's wallet in his pants pocket. They were stranded. All the money was gone; credit cards, gone; driver's license, gone. Everything. They were cleaned out. They had decided to take a year's vacation in their camper, which they had just bought, and of course being robbed like that, that was the end of the vacation for them."

"Are there many thugs about really?" I asked.

"Who's going to count them?" he asked. "I don't know how many there are. But it only takes one to make you cautious of everybody. And you've got to be mighty careful. There was another couple had a similar experience.

"Feller knocked on the door in the middle of the night and said his car had overturned and his wife was trapped under it half a mile down the road. He couldn't get her out and would they help? Well, who is going to refuse a request like that? Off the trailer owner went to help, leaving his own wife with the trailer. He hadn't gone a quarter of a mile before he was held up, beaten, and all his money taken. When he got back to the trailer his wife had been beaten too, the trailer robbed by an accomplice who had been hiding in the dark, and he'd made a complete wreck of the interior. So they were cleaned out too." He paused. "After a while you learn," he said.

"But what are you going to do?" I asked. "If someone tells you there has been an accident down the road and people are dying—surely you must go to help them?"

"Well," he said, "I suppose you do. But it don't hurt to take a gun along if you got one. I had a feller come to my rig one night pounding on the door and tell me his car had gone off the road and was in a ditch and would I help to pull him out?"

" 'Sure will,' I said. 'Just as soon as it's daylight. Meanwhile go on back and sleep in the car.' Well, he went off and then he came back again and started pounding some more and I said, 'Buster, I got a gun loaded with buckshot trained right on you. Now get moving and the next time you come by, you're going to get shot.' Off he went and the next morning there wasn't any car in the ditch and there never had been—not for some miles along the road."

His name was McDowell, he told me. He had been nine years in the Army, he said, and had been discharged disabled, for he had meant to spend his whole time soldiering. Still, he had a small pension on discharge and he heard of a position open in the forestry service for which he had applied. Despite his disability, he had been accepted and had stayed with the forestry service eleven years.

"I could have stayed on a few more years and retired on a good pension," he said. "But time was getting on, and I thought I'd better not wait for the pension but get out while I still had my health. I had enough put by, with the Army pension, to see me and the missus through." He raised his head and looked about at the little flecks of yellow made by the aspen in the dark-green belt of conifers a mile away.

"That was eleven years ago," he said. "We've been camping ever since. We've visited six thousand camping sites in State and National Parks all over the nation. I'm getting a little old now. . . ." His voice trailed off and for a while he was silent.

There were some mountain lion about, Mr. McDowell told me. He'd seen their spoor. And a couple of evenings back, when he was driving through the forest, a deer had dashed terrified across the road in front of his camper, and out of the corner of his eye he had seen the tawny shape of the lion which, balked of its prey, had swirled, snarling, into the undergrowth.

"Where are you headed?" he asked.

"On up into Colorado and then maybe to Yellowstone," I said.

"Anvil heads up there," he remarked.

"Storms?"

"Yes. Bad weather. I'd stay out of there, if I were you."

We chatted a little more, the generator which had in a sense brought us together now forgotten. Camper people, he said, were great readers and had a wide acquaintance with each other. Like ship captains in the old days meeting at sea, campers get together often for a "gab" and to trade books and other comforts. His own favorite was Jack London, and I believe he had read every book London ever wrote. Camping folk, he told me, got to know each other over the years, inquired of each other's whereabouts and to a degree took care of each other. They clubbed together, for instance, to buy a used rig for a man whose camper had been destroyed by vandals and who without it would have had to live in a rented room the rest of his days after having had the whole continent to roam in. They had raised a hundred dollars to get surgical aid for another camper who needed an operation.

"He had a chicken bone in his intestines," said Mr. McDowell. "There was a surgeon I knew and I spoke to him about it. The surgeon said he had to have a hundred dollars—that was the least amount for X-rays and the use of an operating room and the anesthetist and all of that. So a few of us got together and we raised the hundred and the surgeon operated. He didn't charge anything for himself and the patient got well. He went to work at what jobs he could find and he went on working until he paid us back that hundred dollars. He's back with his rig now, doing well."

The children came back from their horseback ride and Mr. McDowell, after being introduced to them, went his way.

"Who is he?" asked Kevin.

"An American," I said. "A real one hundred percent genuine American. Goes where he wants, takes care of himself and his friends, and has no master. In fact, I think if you boiled the hopes of the whole nation down to an irreducible essence, you would come up with something like Mr. McDowell."

chapter

Nine

IT WAS time now to move down into Monument Valley and the Navajo Indian Reservation, headed towards the Dinosaur National Monument, which lies on the Colorado-Utah line.

To get to the Navajo Reservation from the Kaibab forest you descend down U.S. Highway 89A from Heaven into Hell. In the terminology of the map, you go from the Kaibab National Forest, with its lovely cool forests and mountain meadows and its plentitude of grazing and good water, down to House Rock Valley, with its bitter, scoured, eroded land, its massive and forbidding line of sterile cliffs, its grim mesas and baked red earth, and there you are in the Navajo Indian Reservation—which you can drive across for several hours, wondering whether you are ever going to get out of it.

I was told by one whom I thought an authority on Indians, that the Navajos like to live on their sun-parched, wind-scoured desert of a reservation, and that they would be very unhappy indeed if they were moved to the cool groves of the Kaibab National Forest, which is a reservation for holidaying whites. I don't believe it for a moment, and I have heard that story told before. I've heard it told about Welsh miners, for instance. Welsh miners, thirty years ago, were supposed to enjoy living in cramped cottages, all strung together in a row like cells on a prison block, with a pump in the backyard to serve for water—or maybe down at the end of the street—and a basin in the kitchen in which to do all the washing. When a proposal was made to install proper toilets and bathtubs in the miners' cottages, the authorities on Welsh miners, in those days, said that it would make them unhappy, and they would in any case only use the bathtubs as receptacles for the storing of coal. And when I suggested to someone that the Navajos might be given some of the Kaibab National Forest I was told that while they wouldn't store coal in it, they would graze sheep in it and destroy the forest. In fact, it was intimated that it was by overgrazing that their reservation was reduced to such a forbidding place.

Well, the Navajos don't have to graze sheep. Grazing sheep isn't the kind of thing that people have an overwhelming desire to do. The ancient Israelites, for instance, grazed sheep and then went on to do much more exciting and clever things and I have no doubt the Navajos could do the same. The question of the future of the Navajos and all Indians is no doubt complicated and the more experts who study it, the more complicated it will become. But getting to the moon was complicated and we've done that, leaving the Navajos alternately baking and freezing in the desert, raising sheep and selling a few beads. You'd almost think they weren't Americans.

As you see I am angry on the subject of the Navajo and the Indians in general, but the contrast between the white man's world in the heights above, and the Indian world in the desert below is revolting.

It is very hot on the Navajo Reservation—the temperature rose to a 100 in the bus. I wish I had had a barometer with me to get some idea of our altitude, for I think the whole reservation, which extends over several plateaus, is quite high. But whatever our altitude the heat was of the same brilliance and quality as that in Death Valley.

There is a place on 89A where the road takes a sweep around a great bend, along the edge of an escarpment, and from the forested heights you can look out over the reservation below, shimmering in the heat and glinting in tawny yellows and tired reds and pale blues and gray-greens. The Vermillion Cliffs at noon were an exhausted pink and the road ran along their foot in a wearying line stretching to the horizon. It was along this road that we traveled to Marble Canyon and Lee's ferry, which was once the only point for a hundred miles at which the Colorado could be crossed.

It must have been a busy roaring place a century or so ago, for here the oxen were made to swim across the river and the wagons (if the water was high) were taken over on a flatboat. The countryside about is of sandstone—brick-hard and scrub covered. Once across the ferry (by a narrow bridge which was just wide enough to let the bus through) we ran into a windstorm—half a gale, I would say, and gusting up to fifty knots. The wind was out of the west and, since we were traveling roughly south, broadside to the bus, which picked up a little lee helm and had to be oversteered to keep it on the road.

What a wind that was!

It covered the baked red plateau along which we were driving with a thin red smoke of dust, which seethed against the side of the bus like a steaming kettle and had soon reduced the glass of the windows from transparency to translucence. It seethed and whimpered and whined, determined to take the whole Navajo reservation (with which are thrown in the Hopi, on a reservation of their own) and deposit it in New Mexico. We lurched along in this wind, through a steaming cauldron of red dust, thinking what it must have been like in a covered wagon, and how the children must have fretted both from fright at the sound and from the sting of the sand. After an hour of this, with no let up, I saw at the side of the road a sign which read "Dinosaur Footprints" and I stopped the bus immediately.

"What's the matter?" asked Hazel.

"Dinosaurs," I replied. "We're approaching their feeding grounds. You can tell from the musty smell in the air and the swampy squashy nature of the ground." (I was feeling a little light-headed.)

Tich, the kitten, was the only one who took me seriously. She disappeared behind the back of the sofa.

Although dinosaurs are practically everybody's favorite monster, only my boys would get out to look at their footprints. So out we got—Kevin, Christopher, Rory, and Cormac—and battled our way across the seething road and onto the vast cauldron of the desert in the direction of the dinosaur footprints. They were not easy to find at all. There was no marker which located them. We found two other hardy souls poring around in the stinging sand and after a while they gave up, and we located a dubious shallow depression which could have been a dinosaur footprint or a place where a cow had passed by last rainy season.

"Here they are!" cried Kevin, who had gone farther off, and there they were indeed—undoubted dinosaur footprints, perhaps fourteen inches long along the axis of the great toe, and looking remarkably like the tracks of a vast chicken. The sight was astonishing—really and truly astonishing. The more one thought about it, the more astonishing it became. This whole place, this enormous baked shield of hard red sandstone, had once been a vast bowl of soft red mud. By once, I mean in the Jurassic period, say one hundred and fifty million years ago.

All right, we can accept that. And we can accept also that over that vast bogland, troops, flocks, herds, gaggles, prides, slithers, or some other collective of dinosaurs had once roamed. But right there it all becomes unbelievable. Reconstruct it for yourself. Say, for the sake of that reconstruction, that one particular dinosaur, one hundred and fifty-one million, nine hundred and eighty-four thousand, three hundred and twenty-one years ago, say on the fourteenth of October at seven in the evening, waddled at this particular spot on his big scaly feet, his head cocked now here and now there, looking for food or danger, and left a footprint in the mud. And then, right then, the mud, which had been very squishy (you can see this from the way it piled up between the toes), began to dry. And it never rained again on that footprint, at least not until the footprint had been dried out and baked as hard as a brick. No other animals stepped on it or destroyed it. Vegetation did not erupt through it and wipe it out. The wind did not scour it away. The rain did not dissolve it. It remained there, enduring through the ages, testifying that a dinosaur, long, long before Man had appeared in the evolutionary scheme, had passed that way. The dinosaur itself is gone—its bones, muscles, skin, claws, all disintegrated into nothing. The footprint—surely the least enduring trace of it—remains. It is incredible, but it is true, and I wondered whether on some unknown planet we may not one day find no living thing, but only footprints in the baked earth, of things that once lived there.

There were a lot of the dinosaur tracks, once we had

located them. They roved about aimlessly, so that when the creatures made them, they were obviously at ease and not in any degree alarmed. Their resemblance to giant chicken tracks was remarkable. The question arose (with such a wind blowing) of how long these tracks would remain and whether some steps should not be taken to preserve them. But the answer, I fancy, is that the wind will not destroy the tracks. The same wind has probably been blowing, in season, with the same gale force for millions of years, and the tracks have remained.

They are undoubtedly eroded by the wind and by occasional rain, but at the same rate as the surrounding soil and so they remain, just digging themselves down deeper by micro-centimeters, as the surface of the ground is itself eroded away. And there they are, startling and unbelievable —a casual witness to the time when reptiles, not Man, ruled the earth.

I have no trouble with charts at all—or not much except approaching a strange coast on a dark night and listening for the mutter of the sea on half-submerged rocks. But I have a lot of trouble with maps. The two are not the same, of course. Charts warn of dangers and tell of safe places and locate harbors and destinations. How you get there is up to you. But maps are (as we use them) guides for getting from one place to another. And it is my fate that I will lay down a route from one place to another and invariably mistake my way. Then stubbornness sets in, and I will not inquire the right road but cast around with a glance at the sun or the moon to give me direction. Only when hopelessly lost will I stop at a service station and ask to be put right.

I could not afford any mistakes in map reading at this time, however, because I had to get to the Dinosaur National

Monument and then to Salt Lake City, for it was time for Kevin and Christopher to return to Hermosa Beach. I gave Kevin the job of working out the route and we bowled along for hour after hour in that dry wind with the red dust slithering across the road and over the desert. We went past Tonalea and Cow Springs and up March Pass and down into Monument Valley and still the dry wind blew as if there were never going to be any rain again on earth.

We passed on the way a number of little shelters by the side of the road at which Navajo children were selling beads and rings, earrings, polished stones and blankets. The boisterous wind tore and rocked the shelters and the dust fled by, powdering the trinkets and providing a clue as to why the Navajos wear clothing that covers them from neck to ankles. If they did not, they would be sandblasted.

I had to stop at one of these stands because it seemed to me the height of callousness to flee past in our beautiful, sand-tight bus, ignoring these offerings of the children and their attempt to earn some money. The stand was run by an elder girl and her two tiny sisters. They didn't speak English —either because they did not know the language or because they were too shy. As we approached, they seemed to be looking for a place to flee, like frightened deer. They stood their ground, however, in mounting desperation and gained a little confidence as we looked over the contents of the stall, which was a treasure house both of color and of patience. I mention patience because all genuine Indian jewelry or pottery or rugs or blankets are handworked and require many hours of careful labor.

A Navajo rug three feet wide and five feet long takes about three hundred and fifty hours to make on a hand loom—call it forty-four eight-hour days or about nine weeks of work.

A hundred and twenty-five or a hundred and fifty dollars isn't, then, very much to pay someone for nine weeks of work. The same thing goes for Indian beadwork. The beads, if genuine, are still handmade, not bought from a factory. A tiny piece of shell or turquoise is first drilled through with a hand drill; then the little irregular shaped pieces, strung on a string, are rolled on a piece of fine sandstone until they become round or at least cylindrical. This was the technique of Cro-Magnon man and possibly of the Neanderthals before him. It is the way we ourselves would have to make beads if all our technology were destroyed. So you will readily understand why the tiniest Indian beads, being the most difficult to make, are also the most expensive.

I am not an expert in these matters. I bought a book about Indian arts and crafts and I am very glad I did because, looking at this stand of Navajo handiwork, I was humbled and refreshed by the enormous patience which had gone into all this work. It is nice to find people in the world who are not rushed for time, who can take three hundred and fifty hours, for instance, to make a rug, or who can spend half a day scratching a design in hard sandstone in which to make a rough silver casting for a broach. Part of our sickness surely is our abuse of time. We try to use it to the fullest by cramming a dozen activities into a single hour so as not to "waste time." But that is surely the most outrageous waste of time; to destroy it with frantic activity so that time as time has no chance to make its presence felt. Surely time is a lovely slow river, leisured, easy and serene. The happiest people are those who take this view, who are not rushed and who refuse to be rushed. Neither happiness nor success in terms other than financial lies in mere activity. They lie in the savoring of each hour. We tend to approach time like starving men at a banquet. We eat our fill and are surprised that everything should be so tasteless.

We bought a turquoise necklace and one of Indian silver with the squash blossom pendants—an Indian adaptation, by the way, of the small silver pomegranate decoration which the Spanish vaqueros wore on their trousers and capes. I gave the little Navajo girls some candy, hoping they would not think me patronizing or pompous. They took it with fear and no doubt a prayer to their old gods that they should not die from this gift from the white man. When we came away, a dilapidated car, driven by a large man, stopped beside the bus. The owner beckoned me over.

"See you were buying some stuff over at the stall," he said. "You want to take a look at what I got?"

No doubt he was a nice man and kind to his children and a supporter of his church and a payer of his taxes. But right at the moment I despised him. What right had he to enter an Indian reservation and sell his goods in competition with the Indians? Having taken their land away from them are we now to take away their trade?

The man assured me that the Indians would cheat me and I assured him that that is what I probably deserved. He eyed me for a while in silence, decided I was a lunatic and drove off. Across the road I saw the three little Indian children watching me. I hoped that they understood that I had not betrayed them; that I had not bought anything from the man in the car. I waved to them as we drove off and I am sad that I will probably never see them again and they will not know that I am really and truly and honestly on their side. They were soon lost in the wind and dust out on that hellish reservation where I am assured the Navajos love to live.

chapter

Ten

WE ARRIVED in Monument Valley just as the sun was setting. It was the very best time to be there. The plinth-like mesas and Daliesque arches into which the sandstone is carved stood in menacing silhouette against the sunset. Their edges glowed with fire. The clouds, which an hour before had been high strato cirrus—fleecy white and enormouslv distant—now, starved of light, loomed dark and brooding in the sky. And the sky had lost its almost merciless blueness and turned to shades of pale green and buff, of bronze and of red, with here and there still a stain of azure. All these colors peeked through the darkling clouds while night flowed over the flat land.

What is strange about Monument Valley is that Nature should employ the shapes of Man so that there is a confusion in the mind; a lack of separation between Nature and Man; between chance and design. The wind carved these towering pillars, these tremendous square blocks, these graceful arches in the sandstone. But was the wind thinking with the mind of Man while it worked—designing arches and plinths and square blocks? The place has a graveyard feeling, as if all these massive towers and tablelands are what is left of a civilization whose people have utterly disappeared from Earth, and that feeling is summed up in the name—Monument Valley.

We parked the bus to watch the sunset over this place which seems a graveyard of giants. One massive pillar, illuminated in fire, dominated the land. Its shadow was three miles long and its sides and top glowed cherry red. And as that color waned the pillar melted into the night, leaving us staring at nothingness, our flesh raised in goose pimples.

Moab was our destination now, and with time running short, we had to put in many miles after dinner to reach it. You know Moab, of course. It lies east of the Jordan and the Dead Sea; north of Edom and south of Ammon. It was conquered by the sons of Moab, who was himself a son of Lot, whose wife was turned into a pillar of salt. Moab took over the district to which he gave his name by driving out the original inhabitants, who were giants. You can see the remnants of their civilization in Monument Valley. The Dead Sea is a fair piece to the northwest and is now called the Great Salt Lake. Little has been heard of Edom, to the north, in recent times but its warring tribes gather each year at Cheyenne for amusement and profit.

Moab then was our goal and we hurried on towards it through the night and Moab retreated northward before us and so remained unreachable. The hours went by, the miles fled past and still Moab was no nearer.

"How fast are you going?" I said at last to Kevin when midnight neared and Moab still was not in sight.

"Sixty-five," said Kevin.

"That is the trouble," I said. "You must slow down. We

are in another dimension, far, far back in time. Speed is useless. Places such as Moab are not to be reached by haste. Kindly back off."

"Fifty," said Kevin dutifully.

But it was only when we had dropped to forty-five and sung a few mournful songs that we found Moab lying gray and empty in the black bowl of a valley. It appeared as by some witchery out of the void and the darkness. Moab has no outskirts. There was only Moab and then the wilderness with the Edomites howling to the north and the Ammonites making their shrilling, whistling sounds to the south. However, by driving very slowly indeed we found suddenly on our right a dark area in which there were a number of caravans in the form of campers, drawn up for the night, and we slipped into this place and turned out our headlights and turned off the engine and listened. And in the silence of the Biblical night I heard close at hand the gurgle and slap of river water.

"The Jordan," I said. "We will bathe in it in the morning."

But the river was not the Jordan, nor even the Alph headed for caverns measureless to man, which had been my second guess. It was the Colorado, a gray swirling boiling rampaging river of mud, "too thick to drink and too thin to plough," as they used to say. The amount of sediment in it made the water opaque and solid-looking, and the riverbed must at this point be a nightmare of potholes and rapids, for there were enough whirlpools to have turned back Ulysses, though a pleasure-boat came bucketing by shortly after breakfast with some sightseers on board rejoicing in the disturbed waters, which terrified me, who have some slight claim to seamanship.

I couldn't believe that this river was the Colorado and had

to look it up on a map to reassure myself. It seemed to be flowing in quite the wrong direction for the Colorado. Also it seemed to be flowing up hill. But then Western rivers are confusing. They do not course along seemly valleys headed in a businesslike manner for the ocean. Not at all. They rampage about here and there, across deserts and through mountain ranges, digging deep canyons at times, and here and there producing, in the blinding sun and arid land, a grove of willows or some other outrageously out-of-place growth. Occasionally tiring of sun and light, they disappear underground and emerge again miles away. They are, to say the least of them, untidy and untrained; and I will never get accustomed to the sight of rivers, full of swirling and splashing water, running through deserts as dry as bone dust. But the West is full of such contradictions.

I have said little about the bus up to this point because it behaved splendidly. It did just about eight miles to a gallon of regular gas, had ample brakes, steered easily, though picking up a little lee helm in a crosswind because of its size. We had to do nothing to it but put in gasoline and oil and, being now in higher and cooler desert than the Mojave, were not concerned by the fact that the big air conditioning unit did not work.

But Moab put a jinx on the starter. In getting into that dark caravan park the night before, I had several times stalled the engine, for engines will always stall when you are in a hurry or distressed or lying smack across the middle of a high-speed highway. However, I could always restart the engine by turning the ignition key to the "start" position. But after breakfast, when it became time to leave Moab, the starter would not work. I tried it with the gearshift in "Park" and it would not work. I tried it with the gearshift in "Neutral" and it would not work. I tried it pulling the key out just the tiniest bit and then pushing the key in as far as it would go while saying a "Hail Mary." It would not work. I invited Hazel to say a "Hail Mary" while I gave the starter switch a good cuff under what I trust was its right ear, but without result. And if I had not once owned a forty-foot yawl with a sticky starter I would at this point have been completely frustrated.

"It's the solenoid," I said. "It has shorted out." Actually I have only a vague idea of what a solenoid is. But I know what to do with it when it won't work. So we dismantled the little table which was mounted over the engine housing and lifted up the housing and I peered down into the improbable mess of machinery below. As is always the case with engines nothing made any sense for a while. Then I identified the flywheel housing, the gearbox and, over on the port side, a large, round barrel shape which was plainly the starter. I could see no solenoid, but three wires ran down to two terminals on the barrel.

"Turn the ignition on," I told Kevin, and bridged the gap between the two terminals with a screwdriver. There was a wonderful display of sparks and then the engine started. This was our method of starting the bus from then on, for the starter switch would work no more. It had performed its quota and refused to make any further effort. That is a characteristic of starters, and it is shared, as the whole world knows, by anything which is electrically operated. The nature of electricity is one of opposition to human wishes.

and that was the pressing need to dump the contents of our chemical toilet holding tank.

The bus was provided with a clamp-on, flexible hose by which this could be emptied into sumps, which are a feature of many gas stations these days. However, I could not find this hose though I had searched every compartment of the bus and so I concluded that this essential piece of equipment had somehow been left behind. Until it was replaced the only thing to do was to empty the holding tank in the wilderness far away from any human habitation. This I now proposed to do, for the need was urgent.

After traveling some miles up Highway 128 we found a suitable spot, pulled off the road, and with a sense of the greatest guilt, I opened the valve of the holding tank. As soon as I had done so the wilderness in which I had stopped disappeared. Cars began to appear from both directions, full of people violently opposed (as indeed I am myself) to pollution of the Earth. The brilliant blue stream, gushing from the side of the bus on to the parched ground was not to be hidden. The cars slowed down and people stared and went on, composing letters to Congressmen. And that wretched blue Niagara continued to thunder to the ground until it seemed to me that we would very soon have covered the whole of the fair State of Colorado inches deep under a baby-blue sea, with a piny odor that God never made.

At last, however, the cataract diminished slightly, lost a little of its vigor and gusto, diminished still more and was finally reduced to a trickle. I closed the valve as a pickup truck belonging to the state highway department came lumbering towards us. I made a puling attempt at pretending to inspect my tires. The pickup slowed, almost stopped, and went on. I got back into the bus and drove off rapidly from the scene of my horrid deed. I apologize to the State of Colorado and to the whole of America for what I did. My defense is that I had no alternative, and I selected a place far out in the desert. That one spot in the red desert has probably been stained baby blue for all time. I acknowledge that. I admit I did it. But in generations to come it might provide a curiosity for tourists. Perhaps there is some solace in that.

On then to Cisco, which may be where the Kid came from. But first across a very narrow iron bridge over the Colorado, where I had to sight along the girders, as along a gun barrel, to get through without touching one side or the other. The bridge was of iron and it being now midmorning, was very hot. It occurred to me that I might not have been able to cross it at night when the iron would have contracted from the cold and the bridge been narrower. The fit was that tight.

This place was called The Crossing of the Fathers, if my log does not mislead me. And it was here that the Franciscan Fathers, Francis Atanario Domingues and Silvestre Valez de Escalante, crossed the Colorado, trying to find a shorter route from Santa Fe, in New Mexico, to Monterey on the California coast. At this point, about 250 miles northwest of Sante Fe, and most of that desert and mountain, they were almost out of food. That was September 13, 1776. Two months before, thirteen British colonies on the other side of the continent had just declared themselves a sovereign and independent nation. It is a surprise to be reminded that the west has a history as old as the East. The Villa Real de la Santa Fe de San Francisco, for instance, was founded in 1610 so that by the time of the Revoluntionary War it was over 160 years old.

Somewhere around Cisco we left the desert—the vast mass of the Great American Desert which had stretched all the way from Los Angeles to the borders of Colorado, though with fertile highlands between. The air now lost its glass-bright dryness and took on a shade of soft blue which reminded me of the west coast of Ireland. The similarity was astonishing—soft blues and greens and cloud shadow over the fields. And I began to notice a great number of birds with blue feathers (do blue-feathered birds survive in blue-air country in keeping with Darwin's great dictum?) and also a number of magpies.

I explained to Rory and Cormac and Arabella the significant character of magpies the world over. They are by no means ordinary birds, but have supernatural affinities. In Ireland, for instance (and no doubt the same holds true in Colorado), you must say a civil word to a magpie when you see one or you will have bad luck all day and maybe the next day as well. For Irish magpies are but the transformed under-gods of the old Celtic worship. I could not be sure, as I told the children, about Colorado magpies, whether they are just birds or beings, but pointed out it does no harm to wish them well as they flutter here and there, for a man is a fool if, out in the great world, he neglects measures for his own safety. Magpies according to the ornithologists are related to crows and ravens and it is a thing well known that Odin had two ravens, Munin and Hugin, who flew about the world gathering news for him. It is also very odd that ravens are fond of battlefields and have flown over them like black and ragged flags from time immemorial. Beware then of gatherings of ravens. So I told my little sons, for it is important to pass on such lore from generation to generation. Otherwise it will be lost and we will be left to the comfort of computers and electrified tape and that is no comfort at all for these things have no soul.

We were glad, having crossed the Colorado by the tight-fitting bridge, to get back after three hours of rough riding onto a paved highway. Kevin, who had driven in the rough parts, now turned the bus over to Christopher, who up to this point had not been given an opportunity to drive. Meanwhile I became fascinated by the countryside which would certainly have surprised the geography teachers of my childhood.

Perhaps you had teachers of the same sort. They divided the world up into zones in which differing kinds of trees and vegetables grew. There was the tropic zone and the sub-tropic and the temperate and the arctic. In the tropic zone you got coconut palms, bananas, and (with any luck) vast man-eating trees in Sumatra or other forbidding places at whose base lay the yellowed skulls and rib cages of their victims. In the subtropical zone a few palms persisted, but geraniums and olives and oranges came into their own. Farther north, in England and Germany was the temperate zone with lush grasses in summer and beech trees, oaks and other kinds of trees which lost their leaves in winter. Then I think came the sub-arctic zone, where the poor Swedes and Norwegians had to live, set about by gloomy pine trees from which they collected resin to caulk their ships. North of that again was tundra in which many Canadians squished around all day. Beyond that was eternal snow and ice, walrus and Eskimos.

It was all neat and tidy and, visualizing this precise division of the world into its various zones of vegetation and climate, I was fascinated as a boy by the thought of moving from one zone into another—leaving behind the last banana tree and finding, a few feet away, the first orange; or saying good-bye to the last spreading beech and finding on the other side of a hill a forest of gloomy firs, thick with trolls.

Well, it doesn't work that way. There is a palm tree growing smack in the middle of the temperate zone in the garden of a house in Bray, Ireland. You turn right on the Dublin road and there's the palm tree luxuriating in the shy Irish sun. And right here where we were, in the lovely farm country of western Colorado with its air like Connemara and its fields like Devon, there were strips of land infested with greasewood and sagebrush—desert growths, then, which should be in Death Valley, according to my school geography. There were birch and poplar in stately growths, there were herds of Hereford and Jersey cattle knee deep in summer grass and a few feet from them, desert land, barren of everything but sage and greasewood. It was all out of place and slightly incredible. And equally incredible it was to find a marker on the roadside pointing to a spot where a trading post had, but eighty years previously, been exterminated by raiding Utes. The man who ran the trading post was, I believe, called Meeks, and the Utes were after horses and blankets and compounded their misdeed by attacking on the Sabbath. Well, they paid for this and similar misdeeds, for there are now, I believe, but two thousand Utes on the face of the earth and once, with the Aztecs, to whom they are related, they were one of the greatest of the Indian tribes.

As soon as you reach the Dinosaur National Monument, you can tell that you are in a place of history and of drama. First hills and then peaks and magnificent cliffs leap from the earth around you, thrust upward by that mysterious pressure from the west called the Laramide revolution, which has produced the north-south ranges of mountains that are a feature of the whole of the New World.

The strata lie exposed in sharply defined folds on either side, continuous in parts and then suddenly interrupted by an upthrusting of lower rocks cutting across them. In places the older rocks are pushed up over the top of the younger ones, and so tremendous and prolonged was this pressure that around Salt Lake City there are faults or breaks in the earth's crust in which Cambrian rocks, perhaps five hundred million years old, have been forced up and over others from the Triassic Period laid down four hundred million years later, and this overfolding extends in places a distance of thirty-five miles.

My own geology, all book learning, alas, deserted me in this area. The Moenkopi, Chinle, and Shinarump formations got hopelessly mixed in my memory, though I dimly recalled the fossil raindrops in the Newark formation, bearing witness, through a hundred million years, to a passing shower of rain.

Still, here we were entering among these strange cliffs and unlikely hills and entering also the Jurassic era. Across this place the dinosaurs once moved in hissing herds (like lizards they had no vocal cords) and deposited their monstrous eggs in masses of rotting vegetation to hatch. Here were once vast growths of trees and shrubs and thick reeds and grasses (for most dinosaurs were vegetarians) and ferns—not all together, of course, for the trees would grow on higher and better drained ground. The trees were mostly conifers, not unlike those which grow today though the magnolia that once smiled on our Southern mansions, smiled also on the dinosaurs, its vast waxy flowers providing dessert for hundred-foot lizards.

We arrived at the camping grounds of the Dinosaur National Monument a good hour before sunset, and found a spot for the bus by a bend of the Green River with, opposite, a tremendous cliff of sandstone. There was sagebrush all about and some poplars, and the sun was golden and warm. It was a good place to rest.

As soon as we opened the door of the bus, Tich got out and disappeared to hunt among the brush. She could turn, in an instant, from domestic cat to tigress. Kevin got out the guitar and tried a few chords and I went with Hazel and the other children to the edge of the river and we watched the thousand shapes that water makes without ever really altering its position.

Rivers are remarkable in that they belong largely to children. Fishermen along with children retain a love of rivers—others regard them only as barriers to be crossed or sources of spring floods. They build bridges over them and dam them. But children enjoy them. They put feet as white as peeled sticks into the deliciously cold water and squeal with ecstasy. They stare for hours into the swirl of the water looking for the excitement of fish. They throw stones into the rougher parts delighting in the "plop" they imagine they can hear above the rush of the water; or, if the river be smooth, they skim flat stones on the surface. They float sticks, leaves and pieces of paper out into the water and, in so doing, launch the triremes of Nineveh and the galleys of Egypt. They listen to rivers and dream of their great travels through strange lands to the Azure Ocean. In the landscapes of children there are always rivers, and standing for a while by the Green River, I recalled a river thousands of miles away whose surface had the gleam of silver, and whose banks were gilded with wild iris. By that river I had more adventures than ever befell me in all my travels, and I expect when I reach Paradise to find it flowing there.

So we dreamed by the river, Hazel and I, listening to the rush and tumble of the water and watching the swifts skim its surface hunting flies. We returned to the bus for dinner very much younger.

chapter
Twelve

A HUNDRED years and one day previous to our arrival, Major Wesley Powell with a party of ten men in four boats had set out down the Green River to explore the Colorado into which the Green empties. The route proposed would take him through the terrible maze of the Grand Canyon and over rapids and perhaps waterfalls in which he and his party might be destroyed, for all that area was unexplored. They sailed off the map in their little flotilla on May 24, 1869, and they sailed back onto it, having run the gamut of the Grand Canyon and all its perils on August 31, after three months way below the earth's surface. When they got back on the map again there were only six of them left and two boats. One man had left the party early in the venture, and three more left when they found the river going a mile deep into the earth's crust. These last three were killed by Indians when they got to the canyon rim. The six who got through had lived for a couple of weeks on biscuits baked with moldy flour and a few dried apples equally moldy.

But they had walked over floors of pure marble, acres in extent and polished to gleaming by the scouring of river sand. Powell mapped the river as he went and obtained a latitude sight each noon by sextant. He was a veteran of the Civil War—Union Army—and had lost his right arm to a minié ball at Shiloh. He fathered the Ethnological Bureau and the U.S. Geological Survey, and compiled a couple of dictionaries of Indian tongues, but very few people know anything about him. His trouble was that he never massacred Indians or shot up Dodge City or got elected to Congress though he had to become an efficient lobbyist to get support for his plans for land and water conservation, which if adopted would long ago have solved many of the West's water problems. He died September 23, 1902, and as soon as he was dead, surgeons removed his brain. He had bet a friend, Willie McGee, that he had the bigger brain of the two. He was right, as was found when McGee died and surgeons compared the weight of the two men's brains.

Powell can claim for his own the greatest monument of any American—the Grand Canyon. It was he who named all the principal features of that tremendous chasm and the others which led into it. Bright Angel Point was named by Wes Powell and so was the Dirty Devil River, which flows into the Colorado. At Marble Canyon he had walked on those gleaming floors which he described in purple prose in his journal; but Black Canyon, where he spent some miserable hours, is now submerged in the vast depths of Lake Mead. He was of Welsh ancestry and strangely enough his name means in Cymric "pool."

Well, here we were camped at the very spot where Powell had gone sweeping by with his party and that evening, when the sun had gone down, we were entertained at a movie by Walt Disney called, I think, *Seven Against the River* which was a bit more fanciful than a book I had written on the subject several years before. On the other hand it was a bit more entertaining too, particularly the part where Wes Powell's brother decided to shoot one of his companions and another of the band bemused rattlesnakes by spitting tobacco juice on their eyes.

After the movie I tried to sort out for the children the bits that were true from the bits that were fanciful, and Rory and Coco were disappointed that it is not possible to spit tobacco juice into the eyes of a six-foot rattlesnake and then seize it by the tail and whirl it around your head and fling it into the bushes. On the other hand, it may be true. I advance this reservation on the statement of Joe Luon, a carpenter who once worked on my house. He was a quiet, steady, sober man, a good worker and, I would judge, careful with the truth. He came, I think, from Indiana and he told me that he had often killed gopher snakes in Indiana with snuff. The method was as follows. When a gopher snake was found, you reached out towards it with a stick on the end of which you had already placed a small amount of moistened snuff. The snake struck at the stick, got the snuff in his mouth, and in a second or two was quite dead.

"It is astonishing to see," Joe told me. "Worked every time. That snuff stiffened them out like a nail." And it was that phrase that led me to believe the story to be true. For had he been telling a tall tale, he would have said, I think, "like a poker."

There was one other interesting thing about the movie and that was that a number of swifts or swallows (in my boyhood I could instantly tell the difference) had their nests on the face of a large sandstone rock nearby and wheeled about snapping up mosquitoes and flies all during the picture. I asked the ranger on what date they returned each year to their nests, hoping to compare this with the date of the return of the swallows to San Juan Capistrano mission—they are always on time. But he did not know.

Now I must tell you something about dinosaurs and, if you already know all you wish to learn about dinosaurs, I would advise you to skip to the next chapter. A geologist once described dinosaurs to me as the most successful form of animal life ever to have existed on earth, for they reigned supreme for something like a hundred million years. Man, he pointed out, even pushing Leakey's theories as hard as possible, has scarcely been around in recognizable form for two million years and it is doubtful whether there was on earth a mammal (to which class Man belongs) as little as thirty-six million years ago. So the hundred-million-year reign of the dinosaurs is certainly impressive, but I don't think *successful* is the word with which to describe it. The point is that they wound up as dumb as they started, perhaps even dumber. The little fellows who appeared at the dawn of the Jurassic Period and who weren't much bigger than a turkey, were far smarter (measuring brain size against body weight) than the thirty-ton monsters of the late Cretaceous who could peer over a three-story building and were perhaps unaware that a three-story building was before them.

When a creature exists for a hundred million years without the slightest increase in intelligence, then you cannot in my view call it successful. It is merely long-lived, and longevity in a species depends on unchanging environment and, as a corollary to this, zero curiosity. Take crinoids or stone lilies. These strange sea creatures, looking like feather dusters, first appeared in the seas of the earth in the Cambrian Period. They are a not uncommon feature of tropical reefs to this day, five hundred million years later. I saw some splendid examples on the Great Astrolabe Reef off the Fiji Islands.

Adaptation to environment, of course, is the Darwinian theory of success in avoiding extinction. The crinoids, growing in the sea, have had a relatively unchanged environment (or an environment with no dramatic changes in toto, for millions of years). Also, they have no intelligence—no curiosity, no desire for change, no process of pondering, no world within themselves with which to alter the world outside themselves. So they stayed in the sea, adapting slowly to the changes of temperature and salinity and so on. There they are today, still crinoids. But the fish who flopped out onto the muddy banks of Devonian pools and rivers, gasped a little air and returned, shuddering and fascinated by the hostile outer space into which they had thrust their blunt snouts, changed. And in changing they gave an immense and brilliant new direction to evolution, fathering all the air-breathing creatures, reptiles, birds and mammals, which now occupy that previously forbidden atmosphere of gases.

Man has also, like the Devonian fishes, just thrust his snout into hostile space and though now, at this very beginning, he must, like the fish, carry most of his old environment with him, he may evolve into such a creature as can exist in airless space drawing nourishment from interspacial radiation alone. Impossible? Not at all. Three hundred million years ago, man was a fish and so were elephants and bats and dogs. Remember that the next time you plop a newly caught trout into a frying pan. It will add zest to your meal.

There is a mystery, though, about those fish who first poked their dark heads out of the water and tentatively sucked a little air into their gaping mouths. It is this: How many millions of years had been spent in gradually preparing them to survive and indeed thrive in this new atmosphere? It couldn't have all happened in one generation—lungs being substituted for gills in one fish's lifetime. No. There was extensive preparation, and once that is accepted one sees immediately a plan. It was planned that some fish should learn to survive in air, and that immediately brings us to the question which scientists refuse to face: who was—who is—the planner?

I will leave you with the question, for once you perceive its necessity and wrestle honestly with it, you will find the answer. But once the concept of preparation, or readiness for change is perceived, then there is immediately before us the exciting question: Are we like those Devonian fishes, being mysteriously readied now to venture into and occupy the space that surrounds our planet? Is what we believe to be exploration in the interests of science actually a prearranged condition triggered for this century? Here I don't know the answer but I think it is affirmative. We have arrived, I think, at our evolutionary point in which some of us (not all of us) will leave Earth and after terrible struggles and the passage of millions of years will become different beings, and far, far better beings, mentally and spiritually, than we are now.

Am I talking here of Heaven and the evolution of angels? No. I might as well say frankly that I believe that even as we are, we are immortal. But both Professor Julian Huxley and Father Teilhard de Chardin—the one an atheist, the other a priest, though both were men of science—have pointed to the upward course of evolution; how each succeeding species has been an improvement on its ancestry. Although quibblers may say, "What do you mean improvement?" no man of sense has to inquire whether a horse is an improvement over a lung fish or a man, capable of travel in space, an improvement over an ape-like creature not quite up to the task of shaping a stone into a tool.

If my theorizing is acceptable it raises the question of the future of that large section of humanity which remains on Earth. If Man achieves an environment here which is unchanging and which is entirely satisfactory to him (which seems at least technically within our grasp) then evolution suggests he will remain frozen in his present form like the crinoids. He will be Homo sapiens but maybe Homo sapiens deprived of curiosity—a degenerate, then, living perhaps hundreds of years but living without purpose.

Well, I have been skating around too long on this thin ice, and I leave you to boggle with the prospect. It will be a matter of concern for the men of the future, living perhaps in the blue womb beneath the ocean in cities with controlled climates of which we have one or two prototype houses today. Those who have spent two or three weeks in such places below the ocean in a silent, unchanging climate return to the surface, it is said, contemplative, withdrawn and lacking in vigor and aggression. Light seems to irritate them and they have some trouble in adjusting to the bustle and noise of the surface world.

The dinosaurs, to return to them, had, during their time on Earth, a remarkably stable climate. It was warm enough to keep these cold-blooded creatures alive over great areas of the earth for over a hundred million years. They developed variety but remained reptiles. Then, quite suddenly, in a period of a few thousands of years, they became extinct. Obviously a change of climate to which they could not adjust proved fatal for them, and possibly this change of climate was the result of the culmination of what is called the Laramide revolution which produced the Rocky Mountains and the coast range of mountains in North America and the Andes in South America. The rising of these mountain walls in the path of the westerly winds would produce both dryness and an increase in cold. Mountains, it would seem, killed the dinosaurs.

The morning after our arrival at Dinosaur National Monument, right after breakfast, we went to see the fossilized bones of the dinosaurs being removed centimeter by centimeter from the rock in which they are embedded. (A national monument, by the way, is created by Presidential fiat in contrast with a National Park or other preserve which requires action by the Congress. Monuments, as distinct from parks, are concerned with history or science rather than with recreation.) This rock, in which the dinosaurs are embedded, a pale gray in color, is called Morrison formation and it is the stuff which is richest in dinosaur fossils. It is itself the debris of mountains, worn down by wind and by rain into shale and silt and sandstone. At the National Monument there is contained in a shed big enough to house the Graf Zeppelin a cliff face of Morrison formation rock which is a graveyard of dinosaurs.

The bones—tumbled about together in grotesque positions—present to the layman the immediate problem of how these dinosaurs all came to die in the same place and in such improbable postures.

The paleontologists say they didn't die there. They died elsewhere but their bodies, bloated with decay, were swept by floodwaters onto a huge sandbar or perhaps island in the middle of a large lake which became a cemetery for them. There they lodged and over the eons when the flesh was gone, the bones became petrified. They remained thus for sixty-five million years or more until a scientist from, I think, Harvard, searching for dinosaur relics and acting, it would appear, on some form of inspired instinct, dug into the queer-looking hill, on which the shed is now erected, and found, a few feet down, the neck vertebrae of one of these ancient reptiles.

We took a little train (though with rubber wheels to the carriage and not running on track) from a central parking lot up to the vast shed to see the dinosaur excavation. It is all beautifully laid out—the huge cliff before you with the exposed bones still lodged in the rock, and a map or chart of it, identifying each of the bones and the creatures of which they form a part. A man was working on the bones while we watched, tapping carefully with hammer and chisel at the hard rock, and every few minutes a talk was given telling us what we were looking at, how it came to be discovered and what is to be learned from it all. It was intelligent and lucid and had to it the dignity of science. There is an exhibit on the evolution of the dinosaurs on the ground floor of the shed —and it was clear and easy to understand without being written for simpletons. I think altogther that the Dinosaur National Monument is one of the most satisfactory expositions I have ever seen, and having viewed the embedded bones I wanted to see what these creatures looked like when alive—not in a picture but in sculpture or other reconstruction.

Now I had seen somewhere pictures of statues of dinosaurs in stone, life-sized, and had thought I would find these at the Dinosaur National Monument. But I was told, with some diffidence, that they were to be found at nearby Vernal at the State Museum, and since this lay on our way to Salt Lake City, where we were bound, we stopped there.

I think the State of Utah should be ashamed of its museum at Vernal. It isn't really a museum but rather a circus side-show and, while it has some interesting exhibits, others are in bad taste. Dinosaur bones and the fossilized shells of turtles found in the desert can certainly claim to have scientific interest. But the bones of a modern woman and child, scattered all over a showcase—the delicate skulls and fragile ribs, pleading for burial, are horrifying. They are on display at the Vernal State Museum. This sort of thing, to my mind, is mere desecration of the dead, for those human remains have nothing to do with dinosaurs or paleontology or geology. They are strictly sensational. What educational purpose does the State of Utah think it is serving by calling gleeful attention to the hair still clinging to the skull of the dead woman, whose pathetic bones are strewn all over the inside of a glass-fronted case? Once she was alive and had her hopes and her dreams and her fears. How terrible to end in a showcase leered at by hundreds of thousands of visitors a year.

It is all horrible—the more so since it is official; the work of a State of the American Republic. All mankind is belittled by it.

I found myself wondering when I returned to the bus—when are human remains entitled to respect and when are they not? Is the dividing line one of time? Are they entitled to dignity up to fifty thousand years old, and not so entitled if older than that? Or is the division a matter of race or of creed? Could it be held, for instance, that Indian bones are of scientific interest only and not to be accorded the respect given to a white man's bones? Are the bones of Christians to be venerated as relics but the bones of pagans to be put in a sideshow?

I feel myself that all human remains are entitled to respect from all human beings. They may be of scientific interest but they should never be part of a circus. Once at an anthropology lecture, a human skull was handed about the classroom. My seatmate held it for rather a long time and I asked him whether there was something that had especially caught his interest. "No," he said. "I was praying." He was right and he will make a great scientist.

Outside the Vernal museum is the mounted fossilized skeleton of a dinosaur, consisting, it seemed to me, of equal parts of reinforcing iron, metal straps, concrete, and dinosaur bones. It is all painted brownish-red, and looks as if it has the wrong head on it. The best thing to be seen is a group of dinosaurs in concrete, done with taste and skill and donated by the hunters of the State of Utah.

The museum at Vernal gave me a curious feeling of being unsafe—as if I had stepped backwards out of my time into the 1880s when patent medicine manufacturers were poisoning the population with radioactive water, and botulism was cheerfully spread about by manufacturers of sausages. It is a pity that the museum should be so poor, for without any addition to its exhibits but with a deep change of attitude, it could be one of the best in the nation.

We left Vernal for Salt Lake City, taking Route 40 and surprised to see, flanking the road to the north, snow-clad mountains. Marsh Peak and King's Peak glittered sharply in the blue sky, dominating the Uinta range, still coated with snow in these last days of June. Magpies were still plentiful and I saw, fierce in the sky, two hawks hunting above the flow of the traffic, to which they were quite oblivious. How little notice wildlife takes of Man! In downtown Los Angeles,

I once saw an eagle poised on the corner of the State building.

"Skyscrapers are just rocks for eagles," an ornithologist told me later, and ever since I have taken an entirely different view of man's cities, which it turns out are, for birds, just convenient perches.

chapter
Thirteen

UTAH is not a fortunate state for me. I like its climate and its scenery and its history. There is surely no sight in the world to match the Great Salt Lake and, beyond it, that vast desert where speed trials are now held at Bonneville.

(It was at Bonneville many years ago that Mickey Thompson came very close to breaking the world land speed record with a car powered by four Pontiac engines—one for each wheel. He burned out a clutch and that finished his attempt for that year. In the same year and at the same place Donald Campbell had a try at the same record with a monstrous car whose wheels I remember as being about four feet high. He had no luck either. He had hardly got onto the salt before his tanks started spilling fuel and his attempt had to be called off.)

The salt of that desert—glistening white and unbearably hot under the sun—is subject to the most curious tides. In the cool of the morning, the salt is firm and dry and good for speed trials. But as the sun rises higher and higher, a tide rises under the salt and water seeps to the surface—a brown liquid which lies about a fraction of an inch over the top of the salt, making it impossible as a racing surface. I have never heard an acceptable explanation of that tide which answers the call of the sun, not the moon. Some have told me that it is a matter of capillary attraction which coaxes the water upward between the grains of packed salt. But capillary attraction will only work with very tiny tubes and the salt desert can scarcely be conceived of as consisting of billions and billions of tiny tubes with walls of salt. Maybe the salt heats up and heats the water below, which expands and so rises to the surface. Maybe that great dragon of the Norse lands, who caused the tides by sucking in and expelling water, is holed up under the Great Salt Lake Desert in Utah.

This vast extent of saltland is a deathtrap for birds. Migrating across the area, they become thirsty and descend, in the midday heat, to those wretched pools of brine to get a drink. As soon as their feathers are damped with brine, they are as good as dead for they cannot take off again. Even on the roadside you can, at certain seasons of the year, find the little bright bodies of birds which were unable to cross this limbo.

Birds, it seems, often get very thirsty while migrating. I have had a thrush-like landbird come down on my boat eight hundred miles off the Hawaiian Islands. I gave it food but it was water it wanted. As soon as a little water was provided it drank avidly, sprinkled water all over itself and took off again.

But I was talking of my luck in Utah, which is never much good. I got Kevin and Christopher off on a plane to Los Angeles, all right, from Salt Lake City. I was reminded in driving into Salt Lake City, that each state of the Union has its own particular driving style, and I think the greatest difference exists between the driving styles of Californians and the residents of Utah. I am not going to say that one is good and the other is bad. I only am going to say that they are widely different, so that a Californian driving in Utah—or a driver from Utah in California—needs to be exceedingly cautious in order to avoid an accident.

The differences between the two lie in matters of speed, of passing, of making signals or not making signals, and of slowing down. We have a very bad habit in California of passing on either side—left or right—as the opportunity occurs. It is legal to do so but it must be very disconcerting for out of state drivers. In Utah there is a bad habit of signaling for a right turn and then swerving over to the left before making it. I nearly got killed once when I pulled alongside a driver who was going to turn right only to have him move over to the lefthand lane first.

Well aware of the difference in driving styles, I had no accidents in Salt Lake City, and moved on to Ogden, where I decided to find a motel and spend the night so that everybody could get a bath. We found a motel, arranged to get a room and parked the bus in the street outside, and then I ran into my bad luck. I parked the bus, switched off the engine, and got out to look at it. One end was protruding into a driveway. There was room to pull ahead and so not inconvenience others. I had been starting the bus by wiggling under the front wheels with a screwdriver and shorting across those two terminals on the starter. But where the bus was now parked, there was a deep gutter and this was full of water, so I could scarcely crawl underneath with my screwdriver.

I pulled off the engine housing inside the bus, peered down into the dark, located the starter and one of the poles but could not see the other. I thought all I had to do was put the shaft of the screwdriver on that one pole and wiggle it about a bit until it hit the other when the engine would start. I did this. There was a tremendous shower of sparks which discouraged me but I persevered and got more sparks and finally the engine started. I moved the bus a few feet and turned off the engine. When I got out, however, a scarlet river of some vital fluid was flowing from beneath the bus, mingling some yards down with the gutter water. Horrified and ignoring the gutter water, I got under the bus and found that I had cut a hole in the transmission fluid line and the fluid was pouring onto the highway. This was Friday evening and on Saturday very few people work in Ogden.

I got on the telephone right away and called the local representative of the bus manufacturer. Luckily, he was still open and he had a transmission man coming in on Saturday, he said, and would send him around to fix the bus. He did fix it too, quietly and competently, and told me that this particular kind of mishap was by no means uncommon on that model of bus.

But Utah's bad luck was not through with me yet. Hazel used the morning to get whole mounds of clothing down to the automatic laundry in a taxi, and I, with the bus fixed, decided to buy a new ignition switch as I had became convinced that my whole starter trouble came from the ignition switch and not from the solenoid.

I had reached this decision on a solid base of pure ignorance and no decisions are so firm as these. I sought out the bus representative's shop and bought a switch. I had parked the bus carefully by the side of the road and had with me

Rory and Cormac. As I came back to the bus, bearing in mind the peculiarities of the Utah traffic, I noted that while there was someone parked in front of me, there was plenty of room behind me to back up and pull away from the curb. So I got down in the road with the screwdriver and started the bus, and climbed in. I took off the handbrake, looked carefully around and, thinking to double-check, shouted to Rory, "All clear behind?"

"All clear," said Rory.

You know what happened, of course. While I was under the bus someone had pulled in behind. I put the bus in reverse, eased back, and pushed in the radiator grill on a brand-new Chevvy.

I exchanged insurance information with the driver, both of us carefully keeping our tempers, and went on to look for Hazel. I went to four thousand nine hundred and sixty-seven laundromats and she wasn't at any one of them. Finally I went back to the motel and waited and waited and waited and in about ten minutes by a clock and four centuries by waiting time, Hazel arrived with all the clothes nice and fluff-dried.

"We must get out of here immediately," I said.

"What's the matter?" asked Hazel.

"This is Utah and the sky is going to fall at any moment," I replied. So without even waiting to put the nice dry clothes away we drove north out of Utah. I didn't really breathe easy until I got to Idaho and stopped at a fruit stand to buy some cherries.

Although it was now the last of June, it was spring in Idaho. We climbed on Interstate Highway 15 up to a splendid plateau, where it seemed to me the ground and sky were parallel to each other and supported by walls of mountains on the horizons. The white fleeing clouds were matched by white swatches of wind blustering over the fields of green wheat. The hay harvest was just being cut and would likely dry fast in the rush of the wind. The weather seemed entirely new-made, in Idaho, and the flatness of the land, in this high plateau across which we traveled, was a revelation to me. One seemed to be able to see a hundred miles, such was the sense of space—far greater even than at sea where the horizon is but three or four miles away, all walled in by the sky. Far, far ahead lay the sawtooth line of the Tetons and all about were vast fields of wheat and hay, the whole tossed by a rollicking wind while great splashes of sunshine and shadow chased each other across the prairies.

We were headed for Pocatello, a city which we had visited some twelve years before. In the interim there seems to have been an earthquake in Pocatello. After my first visit, which I recall distinctly, I would have been prepared to go before the whole bench of the Supreme Court of the United States of America and swear on the most solemn oath that Pocatello has a narrowish main street which plunges rather steeply down the side of a hill; that it is a nice huddled together kind of town, cozy and somewhat old-fashioned. This, however, is not so at all. In Pocatello the main street does not run down a hill, but on a tableland alongside a railroad track, and the town is not snug and cozy but has the open and wide look of an American prairie town. It is not old-fashioned, but new, and the streets are anything but narrow.

My recollection of Pocatello from that first visit was so vivid that I could paint you a picture of it, exactly placing certain houses and, in particular, a restaurant which is now nowhere to be found. The restaurant is famous in our family as the place where my daughter Patricia (then about four) made her public debut. We had been camping in Yellowstone–sleeping out in sleeping bags and cooking over wood fires. That was in the days before it was discovered that bears at Yellowstone are dangerous creatures and not just good old Smokey without a campaign hat.

We had been doing this for two or three days with our three eldest children and we came down into Pocatello thoroughly dirty and in need of a meal that was not heavily laced with smoke. So we stopped at this restaurant, which was on a hill that has disappeared on the left-hand side of a road which has also disappeared, and since it was a darkish kind of place, we snuck inside and asked the waitress whether we could be seated in a dark corner where we wouldn't invite too much attention. She found a dark corner and we sat at the table, and while I was busy with the menu, Patricia got up, walked to the center of the restaurant, a grimy little tot in disreputable jeans, and smiling at one and all began singing in a loud voice,

"Jesus loves me, this I know,
For the Bible tells me so."

I think there was a move among the patrons to collect a little money for us, and the waitress offered to take a trifle off the bill.

We needed to do some shopping in Pocatello. We wanted to get some steak for dinner and I wanted to visit a trailer supply house and find a hose and fitting for emptying the chemical toilet, already filling up again with its baby-blue, pine-scented sea.

I am sure that you have noticed in driving about the countryside yourself how restaurants, gasoline stations, and groceries all switch over to the other side of the road whenever you are looking for them, leaving your side of the road peopled with rundown boarding houses and empty lots. So it was in Pocatello. On our righthand side was the railroad, and over on the lefthand side were the grocery stores, gasoline stations and trailer supply houses—a new industry this, and growing fast.

After traveling some minutes without finding anything on our side of the road, I saw a large trailer supply house on the other side and decided to make a thoroughly illegal U-turn in the middle of Interstate Highway 15. I stopped the bus, looked ahead, looked behind, and all was clear except for a little tatter on the horizon to the south which I thought might be a party of Blackfoot Indians on the warpath. I put the bus in gear, pulled the wheel hard over and started to make my U-turn. Halfway across the road the bus stalled, cutting off all traffic between Mexico and Canada. The black tatter southward loomed larger and larger and became not a Blackfoot warparty but a truck-trailer combination traveling just a little below the speed of sound.

No time for scrambling under the front wheel now and fiddling around with a screwdriver. We were about to be cut in two by a ten-ton projectile unless the bus started. "Pray!" I yelled and turned the ignition key. And that prayer soared up to heaven and shook the gates so shrewdly that the engine started immediately, and we escaped from the truck-trailer projectile, which had not slacked speed, and got over to the trailer supply house. The gentleman in there had exactly the size hose I needed and exactly the right kind of fitting. Prayer has great power but is not often enough used these days, lucky charms and horoscopes being offered as substitutes. But I assure you that a good solid prayer offered with conviction will not only succeed but make you feel better right away.

I couldn't wait to try out that hose. I drove from gas station to gas station around Pocatello, so strangely changed since my last visit, until I found one with a sump to suit my purposes, and I hooked up that hose and opened the valve and emptied our holding tank. I stood right there in front of everybody who passed by as I did this and didn't feel the slightest bit apologetic or ashamed as I had in the wilderness beyond Moab. When it was done, Hazel, who had come round to look, said, "There's one of those hoses in that cylinder thing over the front bumper." And so there was.

chapter Fourteen

WHILE the Laramide revolution, which produced the Rockies, the Andes and the chain of mountainous islands through the Caribbean, was taking place, there was a great deal of volcanic activity along the western coast of America. I give you this information on the authority of a course in historical geology taught by Mr. Ford, which I once took at El Camino College near my house. It was a good course representing a tour through 4,500,000,000 years in twelve weeks. If I had paid more attention to it, I would be able to tell you much more about this volcanic period and would perhaps be able to paint for you a picture of glowing cones a mile and more high, forming palings of fire along the Pacific coast and pouring Niagaras of molten rock, itself exploding as it rolled along, over the western states as far east as Utah and Colorado.

In fact, layers of ash from these volcanoes are to be found in Arkansas and other central states, and one can imagine the skies darkened by the ash clouds carried by the west wind, and the undersides of the clouds perhaps glowing orange and yellow in the flare of the volcanic fires.

Well, my attention wandered a bit during the volcanic lectures; but I was delighted to find, near the little town of Blackfoot in Idaho, an extensive outcropping of lava from these same volcanoes, cutting a grim swathe through the fields of wheat and hay. And it was surprising to find that the vegetation of this old river of molten rock is that of the desert—sage and creosote bushes growing on the cool Idaho uplands as they had done in the burning Mojave in California. That schoolteacher who once divided the world into climatic zones for me, according to the vegetation, was then once again confounded.

As we headed north, bowling along in this delightful countryside in a northwesterly that would have had me sailing in my boat close-hauled and rail under, and flinging a great smother of spray to leeward, the Tetons rose higher and higher—by far and away my favorite mountains, so sharp and formidable are they against the horizon. Where we were the weather was fair with pleasant sunshine and a cool wind. But over the Tetons a vast storm was raging. One snow-clad peak was beset by storm clouds and plainly it was snowing heavily there though other peaks of lesser degree glinted like Irish gold in the sunlight—(Irish gold has a redder tinge than the lesser gold of other nations).

Here was a fine illustration of one of Darwin's theories concerning weather. During his voyage in the *Beagle* he noted that the mountains of Cape Horn are not very high and lie in about the same altitude south as Dublin, Ireland, lies north. Yet Dublin has a mild climate with very little freezing weather and the Cape Horn mountains are perpetually snow-clad and the whole place has a subarctic climate. Dublin, of course, gets the benefit of the Gulf Stream —that vast warm sea-river without which northern Europe would be ice-clad in winter. Darwin theorized that snow produces snow—the snow-clad peaks cool the air about them causing further snowfalls. And this was precisely what was happening on the noble peak of the Tetons which lay ahead of us. Snow-clad, it had cooled the surrounding air and further snow was falling heavily on it although other peaks on which the snow had melted were clear of cloud and bathed in sunlight.

I told the children about the vast range of terrifying volcanoes, with the sky all lurid with a thousand miles of volcanic ash and also about Darwin and Cape Horn and why it was snowing on the mountain peak ahead and they received all this information solemnly and with politeness. But they were dreaming their own dreams of Blackfoot Indians, and wagons lumbering on creaking wheels behind oxen, and herds of buffaloes following the growth of the sweet grass northward into Canada. In one sense each man is an island unto himself and six human beings though, in a bus, can occupy six different worlds.

We had now left the high plateau and entered a mountainous region, and having crossed the plashy Snake River at Swan Valley, pulled into a pleasant auto court spread out beside the river, with cool grass about to walk upon and pine trees in groves and ferns and wild roses. Obviously this was the place to stay, and we had soon been assigned a spot to park, right by the river where we could hear the gurgle and tinkle of it as it hurried along over its bed of stones, eventually to join the Columbia River and meet the Pacific Ocean below Portland.

Rory and Coco disappeared immediately. There was another little boy with a small cart pulled by a donkey at this place and the three of them immediately became friends. I caught glimpses of them every now and then barefoot on the verge of the river, throwing stones into the water as I had done centuries before, and exulting in the diamond light of the sun on the wavelets and the lovely pattern of leaves and light on a little stony island in midstream. Ah rivers—God made them indeed for children, and it is not the Fountain of Youth that we should seek, but the river of youth. That evening, seeing Rory standing calf-deep in the chilling, glinting water, all the gray years fell from me like an old skin and left me clean again.

Before dinner I went for a walk with Hazel and Patricia and Arabella, along the park-like area in which the auto court was situated. We walked through high growths of fern and of wild roses—lovely, shy five-petaled roses—listening to all the tiny sounds of summer—the brushing of the ferns past us, the minute buzzing and clicking of insects and, high above in the trees, the movement of the wind. I suppose our little walk did not last more than fifteen minutes, and ten would be nearer by the clock. And yet each second was enough to fill a century—not merely occupy it but fill it entirely so that there was room for nothing more than the insect sounds and the wind noise and the five-petaled roses and deep grass.

Tich went with us on this little trek, stealing with delicacy and caution through the ferns, startling a jade-green grasshopper or an early evening moth. She also went down to the river and examined it in disbelief, and then she went out onto a little peninsula and crouched there, stirred by a genetic memory common to felines that told her that in water there are often fish to be had and they taste delicious.

There was only one disturbing note about that lovely auto court at Swan Valley and perhaps I am at fault in seeing it. There was a restaurant attached, a nice cozy restaurant with an aroma of good cooking coming from the kitchen. And around the walls were the skulls and horns of I do not know how many deer of different kinds—trophies for sportsmen and eloquent of the good hunting to be found there—but a graveyard of animals for me. And among these trophies there was a human skull nailed to the wall—or at least a remarkably good imitation of a human skull. On the forehead was written in black letters the words, "Game Warden."

I can see the humor in it from a huntsman's point of view, and perhaps it is I who am sick and not those who put the skull there. And yet I find that kind of humor horrifying, for if the skull is real, that is the relic of a fellow human, and there is too much mockery here of man's dignity, for humor. But then I have odd reactions in this area and object to the Hallowe'en display of skeletons though my children are undisturbed by them. I remember once going to my butcher for a Sunday roast at Hallowe'en and finding among all the meat and bones in the place, a vast picture of a human skeleton, and the association was so strong that I left without my roast.

For all these squeamish thoughts we had a good dinner that evening of the steak we had bought in Pocatello and afterwards I took out my viola and played a few jigs. When that was done, by an enormous feat of concentration, and I fancy a little cheating, Arabella and I managed to beat Rory and Cormac at cards—auction bridge, if I remember right. And then, when all the world had turned dark but the narrow strip of sky above, in which stars appeared only to dissolve as clouds slid by and then appear again, I read to the children from Tolkien's *The Hobbit* and we arrived together at that terrible mountain where Smaug lay sprawled asleep over the horde of dwarfish treasure, including some lovely pieces of elfin silver for which Arabella sighed—and I with her. Then we talked of dwarfs and goblins and fairy mists and great gates barring passages through mountains, and we said our prayers and went to sleep by that tinkling river among the roses and in the deep grasses. One does not have to wait for Paradise. See how it lies about on every hand. You have only to reach out and there it is.

chapter
Fifteen

When we awoke and turned on the radio and had endured the tales of slaughter that constituted the news, I was reminded of Mr. McDowell back in the Grand Canyon. For Mr. McDowell warned us, you remember, of the anvil-shaped clouds up by Yellowstone and said we would do well to stay away from the high country. And the news told of a snowstorm over Yellowstone, eight inches of snow having fallen at the western entrance to the great park, and two snow ploughs being called out to clear the roads for visitors. In July, mind you. The radio warned that it was best to come into Yellowstone by the southern or eastern entrance.

My children, being all born in Southern California, had never seen snow, except Kevin, so they were tremendously excited. When Kevin was small we took him, in winter, up into the mountains of Arizona on the chance that it might be snowing. It was. The sight amazed and frightened him—the dark, brooding sky, the white flakes whirling down out of it, and the ground lighter under its white mantle than the dark covering above. He cowered back in the car and did not want to look. But that was years before and now there was snow ahead in Yellowstone, and casting back in our memories to the hundred-and-twenty-degree heat of Death Valley this seemed impossible. There was great excitement then about moving on and seeing real snow for the first time, and maybe getting out and rolling around in it.

We were climbing now and no pretenses, penetrating into the Tetons, for the lovely Jackson Hole country lay between us and Yellowstone. I don't know what it is about the Tetons that attract me so much. It is something to do with the spectacular ridges the mountains make against the sky—the breathtaking slopes and deep valleys and the rushing water and the pine-clad ridges, now graced with the shy forest flowers. There is a blueness in the valleys which is an echo of the sky and down to the margin of the road, snaking always upward and upward, the wildflowers grew. There were patches of gentian and Indian paintbrush and massive goatsbeard, which I took to be giant dandelions and which of course are not a flower at all. And then there was Queen Anne's Lace, thicker than in a Hampshire lane in May, and goldenrod and larkspur (so shy and small in the deep grass) and also mule's ear and in flooded spots marsh marigolds or something very close to them.

As for birds, the Tetons are a veritable aviary and the birds are more colorful than those I have seen in the deep forests of Trinidad. I don't know the birds of North America well, having always been, in this country, a city dweller. But the birds of England and Ireland I know—the linnets and thrushes and blackbirds and missel-thrushes (the eggs of the latter are pale sea-green, roundish and spotted in rust red, and it is a schoolboy myth that a missel-thrush is halfway between a thrush and a blackbird). All these I knew and also wrens and moorhens and skylarks and plovers, for I was country-bred as a boy and to that I attribute the greater part of my sanity. But these birds of the Tetons were all strange to me—exotic creatures in yellow and black and scarlet and blue and I really think that the Tetons in summer harbor the brightest colored birds of all the world.

Soon, however, I could spare only an occasional glance at the birds and the wildflowers. The road became more and more twisting and the corners so blind that even in this lovely country I took to sounding my horn before entering them. Higher and higher we went with the engine laboring in the raw air and the bends getting more perilous, and then at some unmarked spot we came to a downslope. We had crossed the first ridge of the mountains and it was all downhill now to Jackson Hole. That is how steep they are.

I stayed in low gear on the road down, which proved wise for the grade was steep and the hairpin bends plentiful. Even then I had to set up the hand brake hard and use this, with the bearbox and the foot brake, to slow the bus. And having taken all these precautions to prevent my five-ton bus picking up speed which could not be controlled, we had scarcely gone two miles down the mountain road towards Jackson before the smell of burning brake lining filled the cab. There was nothing to do but stop, hanging over a precipice, and give the brakes a chance to cool off. And so, with infinite caution, we inched our way down the Tetons on that winding road and at last slipped into the wide, grassy valley between the mountains which is the hole in which Jackson is situated.

Jackson is a lovely little town, but it was very full when we arrived and the crowds of people and cars—campers and trailers and mobile homes like ours—must have confused me more than is usual, for I remember visiting a museum on the American West in the town and cannot remember a single thing that it contained.

This being Sunday, we called first at church but were too late for divine service. It was a nice little A-frame type church, with modern stained-glass windows, but though I said some pretty good prayers the starter wouldn't work when I came out. So I crawled under the front wheels with my screwdriver and started the thing up, and to the other tourist attractions of Jackson was added that morning the curious sight of a man repeatedly crawling under the front wheels of a bus with a screwdriver. For some reason the bus kept stalling in Jackson, and matters were not helped by my grossly mistaking the way out of town twice and stalling the bus and cutting off traffic while trying to turn its twenty-seven feet of length on narrow roads with soft shoulders.

However, thoughts of Yellowstone, full of fierce bears and recently powdered with snow, buoyed us up and, Jackson being far too crowded for peace, we started climbing out of the town toward the great park.

We met the first snow at six thousand feet. There it was—unbelievable—carpeting the ground in a grove of conifers. More than that, though the road itself was clear, there was a mound of snow which had been pushed to one side by a snow plough. I stopped the bus immediately and the children rushed out and into the snow, digging their hands into it and kicking it about with their feet and exulting that that splendid stuff of which they had seen so many photographs should actually exist.

For anybody from snow country, of course, it wasn't that great. It was, in fact, refrozen snow, wet and icy. But it was white and cold and you could pick it up in clumps and fling it about, so it was altogether a wonder for those of us who had not seen snow before. Patricia and Arabella scooped some up into a cellophane sack and brought it back to keep in the refrigerator on the bus. We showed the snow to Tich who examined it with distrust and delicacy and tried a little with her scrap of pink tongue.

"Snow, Tich," said Rory. "Remember Death Valley." It was something of a slogan with him like "Remember the Alamo" or "Remember the *Maine.*" But cats are able to take with aplomb those dramatic changes which inordinately excite human beings, and Tich, having satisfied herself on the texture, smell and taste of snow, lost interest in the stuff entirely and returned to the bus.

Yellowstone has so many things to see—from a petrified tree to a 380-foot waterfall, and including Old Faithful geyser and numerous other geysers and also hot springs and lakes of green and blue and yellow and pinkish water—that going from marvel to marvel it is very difficult to get any of them in proportion. It is a place in which to spend a year or maybe even a couple of years. Yellowstone in winter, for instance, with its hot lakes and rivers steaming in the snowdrifts must be a tremendous sight. And what about Old Faithful roaring and spouting high-pressure steam into a frozen and silent world? I'd give a lot to see that. It is my favorite National Park. It could not have been better contrived if Barnum and Bailey had been on the board of consultants together with some great naturalist like John Muir and an artist of the Gothic school like Landseer.

Take, for instance, the little lake that you meet with your first hot springs and geysers as you enter from the south. It is a tropic sea in miniature. No lagoon in Fiji or Tahiti or Bali has those shades of green and of blue; those clear serene waters under a sky of azure. You could sit on the shores of that miniature tropic sea and write yourself a great story of piracy and treasure and the sacking of cities with names like Cartagena and Nombre de Dios and Vera Cruz. You can almost see, at the far end of the lake, the topsails of a big galleon coming out, with the banner of Leon and Castille flying from the fore topmast peak. Or from a cove to the right see the tall and evil prow of a Solomon Island war canoe emerge to the thunder of drums made from hollow trees. And all around behind you is that strange land colored like the icing on a birthday cake and looking somewhat like it too—pink and green and white with tinges here and there of gold and cobalt.

My favorite lake in Yellowstone, however, is tiny Lake Isa. Though you can throw a stone from end to end, it is a lake of distinction for it exactly straddles the Continental Divide, and I think that the waters from one end of it flow, by a rivulet, towards the Atlantic while the waters of the other end flow towards the Pacific. If this is not so, then it should be so and it is one of the things that the nation should attend to as being proper and right and fitting and tending to preserve the balance and sanity of the whole universe.

Lake Isa lies in a hollow to the side of the road with tall conifers growing from little mounds and slopes of hills on the sides—the perfect lake, peaceful and beautiful and not quite to be reached. That the lake possesses qualities of magic was plainly to be seen; for beneath the conifers which surrounded it, the snow lay in chaste mounds, dripping icy diamonds into the water. And just below those frigid waters, yellow lilies bloomed, mystic and wonderful, oblivious to the fact that at Lake Isa the spell of Camelot had been reversed and it was winter that lingered there all year.

Knowing perfectly well that lilies that bloom in icy waters are magical flowers, I was not crass enough to look them up in my little book of wildflowers which I had bought for the trip and which I kept losing whenever I wanted it. But I devised a name for my own satisfaction for those lilies which is *Chrysanthopoloi merlinou nevis.* I will admit that the name is an outrageous mixture of bad Greek and dog Latin, but I could not find the Greek word for *snow.* The translation, if it bothers you, is "Merlin's golden flowers of the snow." Much, much later, when I was no longer under the enchantment of Lake Isa, I did look in my wildflower book and found a flower remarkably like the golden lilies but it was called the Cow Lily or spatterdock, so it obviously wasn't the same thing at all. But doesn't it strike you as extraordinary that somebody could look at a flower, a golden flower, growing among emerald leaves and call it a spatterdock? And are we really compelled to share the world with such creatures whose greatest talent is to turn the battlements of noble castles into mud fences? They've been running the movie industry for years.

Well, we had, of course, to see Old Faithful, who, you will know if you have visited Yellowstone yourself, is not at all as faithful as he is supposed to be. He gushes at only roughly predictable intervals, and yet what a showman the old fellow is! When we arrived, we were lucky for the next display was expected in but half an hour. So we got a good position on the wood duck walk around the crater and, cameras ready, waited while the hook-nosed crater brooded out there on its mound, sullen and quiet.

When you have looked at nothing for a long time, then even the slightest something is tremendously exciting. And Old Faithful knows this. We stared for ten minutes at the nothing of his deformed crater, and then Old Faithful allowed a wisp of steam to escape. It was not much more than you would get from a kettle coming to a boil, but people tensed and exclaimed "Aaaah" and drew back a little. For this was not ordinary steam but steam from a terrible caldron below whose fires have burned since the creation of Earth. Again there was nothing and then, after a while, another wisp of steam, this time followed by a glob of thickish fluid in the shape of a dumbbell which plopped back into the deformed maw from which it came, making everybody tense. Then again nothing and then two or three spurts of steam escaped and another glob of fluid and then majestically and powerfully a plume of steam rose and built up higher and higher, all the time roaring furiously, until it dominated the whole universe.

Arabella, Rory and Coco came closer to me and we stood there in awe while that huge, thundering plume bellowed its primeval roar of defiance and then slowly dwindled back to the menacing nothing from which it had sprung. What terror that sight must have produced in the first man to come across Old Faithful! I can imagine him rushing back to his fellows, through woods and bracken, and crying out, "A dragon! A dragon! There is a dragon just over the hill!"

Yellowstone Park is actually a volcanic plateau with an average height of eight thousand feet, lying between mountain ranges and dominated by Electric Peak in the Gallatin range, named, I believe, after that remarkable Swiss emigrant Albert Gallatin who became Jefferson's Secretary of the Treasury. Apart from the spectacular volcanic displays (and the place called the Fountain Paint Pot is really spectacular, having pools of all those childish gay colors that Walt Disney used in his early cartoons) there are noble mountain meadows bounded by groves of lodgepole pines and carpeted with gentian and cinquefoil, grass of Parnassus, buttercups, redbells, monkhood and larkspur. There is an air of silence and of grace in these tremendous mountain meadows, and it seemed the most natural thing in the world, glancing to the side, to see a tall elk moving through the grass and, at another place, a herd of deer browsing while a stag stood sentinel to one side.

But no bears, to the great disappointment of Rory and Coco. The rangers must have shooed the bears out of the park, for, as I have said, there were plenty of them the last time we were there. They raided the garbage dumps at the camping places and stole our lunch off a picnic table and blocked the road a couple of times. But this time, though it was midsummer, only Tricia saw bear and that for but a moment. Actually the bears of Yellowstone have become a menace in recent years. They have lost their fear of man while retaining the uncertain temper of bears, and have killed two or three people.

Apart from that lovely little tropic sea that one comes across on entering the park from the south entrance, Yellowstone has a real sea in its vast lake, which is twenty miles or more long on one axis and fifteen on the other. Out of this flows the Yellowstone River, which, cutting its way through a mountain range, forms Yellowstone's own Grand Canyon, whose banded walls in many colors are a thousand feet high in places. The walls of the canyon have that cake-icing coloration found near many of the parks, four thousand hot springs, and one hundred geysers. There are pinks and salmons and deep reds and even blotches of green and of blue and orange. But the geology of it all is beyond me, and also beyond me is any explanation for the presence of all that scalding hot water under the ground—eight thousand feet above sea level.

Plainly the water is trapped there and heated by the volcanic activity below but what are the nature and extent of the trap or reservoir I do not know. Old Faithful, I should have said, throws its spout of steam and water to a maximum height of a hundred and thirty feet, and there is elsewhere (I did not see it) a geyser which first erupted in 1928 and put out a prodigious quantity of steam and water in columns a hundred feet high and flung it in all directions. This newest geyser erupts twice in every twenty-four hours, but its eruption periods last for three hours or so, and it makes, I am told, a splendid roaring noise.

Now plainly the eruptive forces behind these geysers is steam power which builds up until the pressure can no longer be withheld. But what is it that permits this build-up? There must surely be some kind of a valve which will only open when a critical pressure has been generated and which closes when the pressure drops below that point. A huge boulder, do you suppose, in a funnel? Or a flat paving stone of lava that flips up to allow the steam and water out and then closes again? I could find nobody who knew.

For so spectacular a place, it was rather a long time before Yellowstone was surveyed and mapped. The reason, I think, was that people refused to believe the accounts of the travelers who stumbled across it. They are not to be blamed, I suppose, for travelers' tales are rarely credited; and when John Coulter, who first stumbled into Yellowstone while taking refuge from hostile Indians, got back to safety to report vast geysers erupting out of a birthday-cake landscape, I have no doubt that people shrugged and concluded that the loneliness of the mountains had finally got him. Coulter visited Yellowstone in 1810—Jefferson had retired only a year previously from the White House and would have been delighted to see him.

The next known white visitor to Yellowstone was Joseph Meeks, a trapper, who got there in 1819. I am not sure whether he is the same who was slaughtered by the Utes as I mentioned previously. Jim Bridger was through Yellowstone a number of times and it was from his account that the first accurate description of Yellowstone was put down by Father De Smet, a Jesuit missionary. I think I saw Jim Bridger's grave in Napa County, central California, behind a tall iron fence, and I thought at the time that he had to die before they could put a fence around him. But it was not until 1870 that a real survey was made of the area, the place accepted as reality, and a start made on turning it into a National Park. It is still slightly incredible. The falls, the geysers, that huge inland sea eight thousand feet in the air, the hot springs, the multicolored earths and salts, the noble mountain meadows—all these, even while you are among them—have the quality of a theatrical backdrop. The mind gets a little numb and you can go past a spectacular cluster of hot springs with scarcely a glance or, seeing the whole earth steaming to your right or left, merely continue on your way.

We lingered a while in Yellowstone, visiting geysers and lakes and canyons until our minds were quite numb with such sights. Then we went out through the north entrance, pausing in a lowering shower of rain to examine Mammoth Hot Springs, with its walls of bitter salts—pinks and blue and gray and white, crowned by wreaths of steam. At Gardiner just outside the park the rain started to fall in earnest and we had dinner and did some shopping in a curio store, a kind of store my family cannot resist.

I wanted to buy a pair of Indian moccasins and Hazel, who is part Indian (there is Cherokee on her father's side), said she would find me a good pair. Now I want to tell you something about moccasins which will save you a doctor's bill and thereby, in itself, justify the purchase price of this book. If you are accustomed to walking around with heels to your shoes, do not throw away your shoes and start wearing moccasins. You will wind up with a broken back, as I did. Hazel, having examined every moccasin in the store, bought me a fine pair made of deerskin and made by the Minnetonka Indians (or so it said on the sole lining). They were of deerskin and beautifully soft and I wore them day after day, fair weather or foul, and finally developed such seizure in my back that I could scarcely get out of a chair. The explanation was that my standing and walking posture was changed by the lack of heels, putting a heavy strain on muscles previously little used. I have had this trouble previously so did not go to a doctor about it but took one of his green pills and one of his yellow pills and put away the moccasins, and my back was soon restored to its full strength.

Since I am a friend to Indians, of whatever tribe, and think that perhaps the world might be saved by a strong bond between the Indians and the Irish (who stand ready with plenty of advice and lots of experience on the rougher side of living), I do not want to cause a fall off of the sale of moccasins. So by all means buy yourself a pair, but don't wear them all the time, at first, but only for short periods. Or if you want to wear them all the time—and society will permit you—buy a pair with heels. The Minnetonka Indians now make these, being quite prepared in the liberality of their nature to adapt their traditional footwear to the peculiarities of the paleface. More, I might add, than we palefaces have ever done for them.

chapter

Sixteen

IT WAS evening then when we left Gardiner and headed northward until we came to Livingston, where I thought I could find an autocourt, for everything elsewhere was full. But I could find none and, the northern night lingering on, went on to Bozeman, which was a mistake for at Bozeman, without in the least planning it, I came on a vast freeway and was soon bowling along this concrete runway at seventy miles an hour. This was no more fun than driving around Los Angeles.

We got off as soon as possible and lost our way in a country lane, for night was now setting in, and blundered about here and there, backing and filling and exercising the Christian virtue of patience until it had worn so thin you could see right through it.

One of the troubles, of course, was that the bus kept stalling and then I had to crawl out with that screwdriver and short across the two terminals on the outside of the starter housing. As the light waned that got more and more difficult to do, and that immense fund of patience which has endeared me to my family and my friends began to run out and to be replaced by profanity.

Finally we got, by a side road, to Three Forks, Montana, which is quite a piece from Yellowstone and still I could find no camping site. At Three Forks I found a policeman at a gas station and asked him whether there was anywhere I could park for the night. And he told me of a side road where trailers parked, and after only an hour of casting around I found the side road and wearily brought the bus up alongside a margin of deep grass. We had driven far too long into the night for any reading or card playing or tunes on the viola. All hands made up their berths and soon we were all fast asleep and slept until deep into the following morning.

There was now a problem of servicing the bus before us. It had been new when we took it over and we had promised Mr. Ricard back in Santa Monica that we would have it thoroughly serviced at the two-thousand-mile mark, which was now approaching.

Butte seemed the likeliest place to do this and we left the bus at a gas station on the outskirts of that town and went on foot into the city to have breakfast and look about. Even on the kindest view, Butte seemed a drab little place or maybe we saw only those parts of the city bordering on the industrial and highway area. On the northern outskirts we could see the vast mounds of the copper mines, which are worked to depths, I believe, of over three thousand feet. At one time the processing of the ore produced such noxious fumes that all the vegetation about Butte was killed off, but now the processing is done at Anaconda and Great Falls and the Butte air is clear and trees flourish again. Nonetheless, the city seemed depressed; the stores, such as we saw, poor and the sidewalk along the highway on which we traveled a mile or so into town and back again, buckled and broken in many places, perhaps from subsidence due to mining.

This air of depression and hardship, bordering on poverty, seems a common condition in mining towns wherever they may be—in Yorkshire or Montana. I did, however, find one novelty in Butte and that was an electric company with an Irish management—to judge by the names of the proprietors. Now between the Irish and electricity the Lord has set an enmity or at least a misunderstanding difficult to resolve. That is my experience. I knew an Irish electrical engineer down in Trinidad, British West Indies, who was in charge of power poles and other contrivances for carrying this mystical influence from place to place and he had the conviction that electricity is not really subject to any rule discoverable by man.

"There's something else in it," he used to say, removing a cooked pelican from a high tension line. "It will leap at you when you least expect it and when the book says it isn't there. I've had more frights from electricity than I have from Germans—" he was a veteran of the First World War "—and I am of the opinion we were better off with whale oil."

I do not get along any better with electricity myself, and I knew a fellow in Limerick who wouldn't have it anywhere near his house, for he said it frightened the cats out of their wits and gave him a toothache. So it was a big surprise to me to see an electric company flourishing in Butte, Montana, under an Irish management.

"If we Irish can lick electricity," I said to Hazel, "we can lick anything." And so I believe.

We were now in the midst of the Rockies, right on the

spine of that tremendous range whose height is perhaps not as spectacular as its extent. We had also passed through one of those invisible walls that divide the different areas of the world from another. Where we passed that wall I cannot say exactly, but up to the time of Ogden I had the feeling of being in the American West, and now we were in the American Northwest. The difference? I think a lot of it lies in the color of the sky. The Western sky—the desert sky, if you will—is of a paler blue and has a kind of brittle quality; hard, often cloudless, and blinding in its light. But the Northwestern sky is of the blue of the Virgin's mantle and landscaped with cumulus. There is more sunlight and shadow about and more softness, by which I mean shadow and sunlight merge and have no knife edges.

Also the trees change. We had met pine at the Grand Canyon forest, but here were mountains clad with pines (lodgepole pines, I think) and every one of the same height to within a foot, like so many stalks of wheat. And as we pulled out of Butte, following along the Clark Fork of I do not know what river, we passed time and again through those changes of vegetation which are always such a surprise to me. For instance, we would pass through a whole forest of pine and then there would be at some otherwise unmarked spot a switch to cedar, and then another switch to fir. The road (it was Highway 10) followed the river down through a gorge and through a series of national forests, beautiful places, preserved, I trust, for all time and on one side of the gorge were pines and on the other Douglas firs. One explanation might be that these are forests planted by man but they were too extensive for such an explanation surely.

We drove all day through them, on the Pacific side of the Rockies now, breathing, I fancy, a little ocean salt in the air, though so far inland. Down and down the road wound, off the spine of the Rockies through a gorge, with the tumbling Clark Fork of an unknown river (Columbia, would you say?) splashing alongside us. This was the Lewis and Clark Trail that we were following, in itself a sign of having left the Southwest for the Northwest—and as that Clark Fork grew in size with each descending mile I wondered, as Clark and Lewis had wondered, no doubt, whether it was deep enough for canoes, or whether to stick to horses.

In my imagination I was soon not traveling in a bus at all but was staggering along, on foot, by this river, wondering whether there was enough water over the boulders yet to float a canoe weighed down with men and provisions, and whether the Indian with me told me lies all the time, half the time, or only when it pleased him.

The transition was quite easy to make and I could see the Indian quite plainly. He was of that kind called Flathead, "through the habit of these people of binding their infants to boards the better to carry them about, in which condition the child lyeth until he is of a year or more's growth, all the time fed from the paps of the mother which from this over-nursing (as well I suppose as the heavy labors they undertake) hang down like the ears of a water dog. Of the women there are three degrees, viz., young maidens. . . ."

"That's a Stop sign," said Hazel, and my Indian disappeared and the moldy deerskins I was wearing disappeared also, leaving me clad, to my surprise, in pants and shirt from Sears, Roebuck.

"Why have you taken to moving your lips while driving?" asked Hazel.

"I was talking to a Flathead Indian," I replied.

"What did he say?"

"He said we should stick to the horses. There isn't enough water in the river for canoes and there are many rapids ahead. I think he's lying."

But the Indian was speaking the truth because later on we came to the following on one of those historical markers which are such a delight for the voyager. It read: "Extract from Clark's Journal. The road through this hilley country is very bad passing over hills and through steep hollows and falling timber. Cross a mountain 8 miles without water and camped on a hillside on the creek after descending a long steep mountain. Some of our party did not get up until 10. Party and horses much fatigued. 12 Sept. 1805."

They got those horses from the Shoshone and their guide was a Shoshone. But he looked more like a Flathead to me.

Have I mentioned that on this road descending from the back of the Rockies we passed through one National Forest after another? We drove all day through these beautiful woodlands, with their disciplined trees which kept entirely to the same size so that one would not stand out over his fellows, and with the Clark Fork of that river (if I say it was the Columbia, it is bound not to be) on our port side. Clark in that little extract from his journal called it a creek and without a doubt he wasn't about to make more than a few miles in the course of a day while I was knocking off scores.

But it soon was deep enough, in my opinion, for a canoe and I started thinking what a fabulous adventure it would be if one were to follow the whole Lewis and Clark route to the mouth of the Columbia in a manner as close as possible to their own. What fun to take a flatboat from St. Louis, up the Missouri-Mississippi and go up with a square sail (when the wind served) and with oars when it did not, against the current! Well, I will do it when I am a little older and have more patience.

A great river for fish, that Clark Fork must be, for there were fishermen in numbers along its length. But it is a turbulent river, whatever the extent of its trout pools, the bottom all boulders and many of them granite. There were a great number of rapids. We must have passed a total of fifty miles of them, with the water splashing white over the rocky bottom. But there were also the loveliest little spits of pure white sand, usually after a passage of rapids, where men could camp in perfect peace in the quiet of the evening.

At Hellgate Pass, through walls of rock, geology overcame history, and I stopped the bus to have a look at the rock. Granite it was, pushed up from the hot maw of the earth and flecked with feldspar and mica. But there was also a great deal of a buff sandstone about, the remnant, I would suppose, of other mountains long worn away. I found no limestone or chalk or anything marine in origin and I do not think that this area was ever long under water though the Laramide revolution overthrust many of the lower rocks to cover the newer marine deposits.

A great number of camping spots offered, but it was so pleasant driving by the river in the sunlight through the forests that not even the children wanted to stop. Also they like swimming pools and we had not come up on one since the Grand Canyon. So whenever I suggested stopping, there was mention of how nice it would be to find a swimming pool, and on I went and then, at the hamlet of Lovell, we came upon a lovely meadow close to the river and laid out as a most handsome trailer park. The sign said "Swimming Pool" and there would have been a most bloody revolt if I had passed this place by.

So there we stopped and it was a very handsome place indeed, surrounded by forested hills and with lush grass to stroll and play on, and electricity laid on for every camping site. When you bring a yacht into harbor, either to a mooring or into a dock, other yachtsmen and sailors gather around and watch to see how well you can handle her. And the same is true of buses and trucks and trailers among camping people.

Ours was the biggest vehicle at this camping ground and several other campers gathered around to see whether I could back it up rightly to the appointed spot or whether I would run over the electrical outlet and perhaps plunge them all into darkness for the night. I did quite well and that is unusual, for normally I make a very poor showing before an audience. I once stuffed the bowsprit of a forty-foot ketch into the cockpit of a neighboring schooner trying to make my dock under sail; and another time, caught in a crosswind, with no sail up, I took the stern pulpit off a rather ugly cabin cruiser when my auxiliary engine failed.

But I did all right with this vast land yacht of mine, despite the tendency of the engine to stall under pressure, which would have necessitated me crawling underneath with that screwdriver. And when we were properly docked and hooked up to the electricity, Patricia, Arabella, Rory and Cormac in a moment got into swimming gear (in a great scurry, with clothes flying left and right), and plunged into that delightful pool with all the zeal of penguins.

Hazel and I telephoned Kevin back in Hermosa Beach. We planned, before the charter on the bus ran out, to have a week of surfing on the Pacific coast if he could get away from his work. All was well with him and Christopher, and both were looking forward to perhaps getting away for that week-long surfing trip.

There was a store at the trailer park, and hanging over the desk a real treasure—a handmade genuine American violin. It was carved out of local cedar. The pegs were hand-carved and also the tail piece and the finger board, and the cashier said it was for sale for sixty dollars and I could play it if I wished.

I took it down and, lacking a bow, tried it by plucking the strings. The tone was quite good and I was sorely tempted to buy it. Sixty dollars, of course, is nothing to pay for a handmade instrument but it is a rather large sum to part with out of vacation money. So I did not buy it and I should have. It is probably the only violin in the world made entirely of cedar though by no means modeled on a Stradivarius. But handmade. A machine-made fiddle costs a hundred dollars these days.

There were birds singing everywhere, it seemed, in the meadow by the river, their song mingling with the high-pitched tinkling of the water. Not a breath of wind stirred and the clear, clean air seemed itself to be resting in that lovely place. We turned Tich loose and she played games of great excitement, stalking all kinds of imaginary prey in the grass, and the sun had gone behind the mountains and the river midges were beginning to gather in their little swarms before I realized that the children were still in the swimming pool and went off to get them.

Nobody that evening wanted to turn on the radio and the word *television* hadn't been mentioned for ages and ages. Tich returned from her adventures to settle on Arabella's lap and eat a few peas left over from dinner, for that kitten has strong tendencies toward vegetarianism. A little wind came up, touching the tops of the pines and flowing over the meadow. I lay in bed thinking that the wind was light enough to send up the big topsail over the main gaff and was thinking of calling Kevin and doing so when it occurred to me that I must be asleep. So I did not bother.

chapter

Seventeen

THERE are many similarities between voyaging by bus and voyaging by boat and, of course, many dissimilarities. On the bus, as on a boat, everybody had certain storage space allocated to him and was not allowed to use any other. Everybody had to put his things away when they were not in use, so as not to produce a clutter annoying to others. Hazel and I took two on and two off—half sea watches—at the wheel, and we found we had to keep an eye on the wind, for in squally weather the bus would fall off downwind a little if you didn't watch it and reduce your speed.

Rain called for the same increase in caution as a rising sea, and though the generator still was not working and never would work during the whole voyage, I still checked on the gear each day as I would on shipboard—looking mostly at the oil level in the engine and the water level in the batteries and in our tanks.

Bunks were made up tidily at the start of each day and, to ease matters for the cook, everybody ate at the same time —Tricia did a great deal of the cooking and did it splendidly.

This is the shipboard and camper routine of people living together in limited space. It makes for general content and happiness if decently observed and it is a great improver of even the best characters, making everyone considerate of his neighbor—which is the basis of civilized society.

The dissimilarities are obvious and were largely to the good. Take rain. On land it is at most an inconvenience. You can get out of it and, though it adds to the hazard of driving, the driver doesn't have to get wet. Many times at the wheel of that bus I luxuriated in warmth and dryness thinking of sitting at the wheel of my boat during the night in driving rain which managed always to find a way through my oilskins and trickle down my back. Then take night itself. At night in the bus we pulled into an autocourt or a trailer park or off the side of the road, battened down, ate dinner and went to sleep. But at night on a sea voyage, the vessel continues on her way, and you sit in the great darkness of the ocean with the constellations overhead—Pegasus perhaps, or Orion, depending on the season—and you do not think great thoughts as you should of the insignificance of Man and the vastness of space, or of the depth of the ocean and the size of your ship, or of what it was that Zarathustra spake that so agitated Richard Strauss.

No, not at all.

You think how odd it is that at night time all clocks run very slowly so that the night, though it may be measured as twelve hours of darkness against twelve hours of daylight, is actually about eighteen hours of darkness, most of which are crowded into your trick at the wheel.

You do not ponder worthwhile matters, such as what you have done with your life to date and what you ought to do with what is left of it. You ponder whether, when you are finally relieved of your trick at the wheel, you will linger long enough in the galley to fix a hot cup of coffee or whatever you will, or just shuck your oilskins and roll into your bunk, and feel that great ease of rest trickle through your aching body and mind.

I have often thought, in setting out on a sea voyage, that I will use my leisure time to catch up on the heavier reading for which there seems neither energy nor opportunity on land. I have carried books to sea for this purpose. But I have scarcely read more than a chapter of them. Sea and sky, changing always, yet always the same, produce a kind of spiritual trance which inhibits deep thought. One accepts and receives but does not ponder. The ocean and the heavens are philosophy enough and man melts into them, becomes, I think, only a part of a greater whole and incapable of separate thought. By which I mean that at sea, you think like the sea and are part of it.

What I am leading up to here, however, is not metaphysics but laundry. Laundry is a continual problem at sea, tended to at odd moments and with but mediocre results. Washing clothes in salt water is a waste of time, for not only will they not get clean, but the residual salt will attract moisture from the damp ocean air, so that they will never get dry. I have at times been driven to the extremity of trying to dry clothes in an oven at sea and that was a waste of time, for they burned at the bottom and stayed damp on the top.

But laundry when you are making a bus voyage is delightfully simple. You just pull up at a laundromat and in an hour or two everything is clean and dry. Hazel, on awaking the following morning in our lovely meadow trailer park at Lovell, announced that she and Tricia would do the laundry and the whole morning was spent on such leisurely housekeeping chores. Arabella, Rory and Cormac, of course, went swimming, and everybody was able to take a hot shower and I even had another go at fixing the generator, not with any hope of success but thinking to improve my character by not giving up. It remained, of course, unfixable. After that I looked over the road maps and decided to go into Idaho to Kamiah and then up to Nez Percé, where I hoped it would be possible to see some Nez Percé Indians.

The Nez Percé were especially friendly, I believe, to Lewis and Clark on their exploration, and were promised in return the protection of the government. In the event, the promise did them no good. Their lands went and, though they fought gallantly under Chief Joseph for their rights, they were eventually defeated. They live now on a reservation and are, I am told, increasing in number. But at the height of their power, when they met Lewis and Clark, there were only six thousand of them.

The laundry done, and the children, including Patricia, retrieved from the swimming pool, we followed the Lewis and Clark trail for a while, through the continuing forests. The river was much wider now, the rapids less, and there were many more of those delightful sandy bays in which to camp. Then we left the trail to pick up Highway 12 to get to Kamiah. A lovely little place we found it to be, its houses tall and of wood with wooden shakes for roofs and all of them with the air of being a hundred years old. The streets were wide and sunlit, built for wagon traffic on market day, I would say, and there were several little children with the dark skin and lovely blue-black hair of Indians in the streets. But whether they were Nez Percé or not I do not know, for we were all of us too shy for conversation.

I mailed some letters in this tiny town in a post office

where the clerk was behind a grill in case of attack and there was a wonderful nineteenth-century atmosphere compounded of mahogany, leather and silence. I would have liked to find a store to buy some souvenirs—something really Indian from the Nez Percé Indians, whom the French named in the mistaken impression that they put ornaments in their noses like the islanders of the South Seas. But I could find no such store, for Kamiah has not yet discovered the tourist trade.

The road to Nez Percé was unpaved—State Road 64—and climbed up the side of steep hills of lava, twisting and turning, getting higher and higher with each mile and all of it delightful. It was so narrow that in places we had to back up to let other cars pass, and on the lefthand side, the ground fell steeply away into that grassy valley, embroidered with wildflowers, in which pleasant Kamiah lies. We reached an airy plateau at the top with wheat fields all about. The ground here was level and in a little while we came to Nez Percé.

The name only of this pretty town is Indian. The rest is agricultural American with an air of farm wagons and horses and livery stables. We were hungry, for all that housekeeping in the morning at Lovell had taken a great deal of time and, adding the travel time to it, it was well past midday. Normally for midday lunch we had sandwiches, but there had been agitation for a little while for hamburgers so we stopped at the hotel restaurant and had hamburgers there.

We were served by two lively and happy girls who took an immediate fancy to Coco, for he has numerous freckles which make him look like the little boy on everybody's calendar. These two girls were of great presence, weighing, I would judge, in the neighborhood of a hundred and eighty pounds each, and that I believe the result of having at hand, and immediately available to them, large quantities of soft, smooth lovely whipped potatoes. This was their favorite food, no doubt about it, and I ask you was ever a greater temptation put in the way of two girls desirous of losing weight? Time and again I saw them pass by that big stainless steel pot of those lovely whipped potatoes with faces set like iron, only to have them come back half a second later for just a little dab on the end of a knife or a fork or a spoon or whatever lay handy.

Their intake (under tremendous resistance) must have been several pounds a day and the result showed in their figures, which were entirely substantial. Coco, they decided, should have some of this favorite delicacy of theirs, and they gave him plenty which he did not eat (though for politeness he took some). One of them sighed, I think at the thought that there should be in the world a human being who did not like whipped potatoes and therefore did not have to struggle, hour by hour and minute by minute to keep to a reasonable one hundred and eighty pounds.

One asked whether we were going to Lewiston and, on my replying that we were, said she had been there herself only a day or so before. She offered no further information of what had taken place or why she had gone. To go to Lewiston was in itself an achievement which did not require embroidering.

Although we were still several thousand feet above sea level the day was very hot, and we were grateful for the quantities of ice in glasses which these two good-natured girls gave us—with even more for Coco because of his freckles. We roamed around Nez Percé a little, enjoying the quiet of the place and the nineteenth-century air and lovely well-kept gardens full of flowers and then, having filled up with gasoline, moved to go to Clarkston and Lewiston and

Walla Walla and then down to Pendleton, having in the course of three hours touched on three states—Idaho, Washington and Oregon.

Pendleton, of course is where those checkered shirts and blankets come from, but I did not look for any of them, for I long ago discovered that you cannot buy coals in Newcastle. From Nez Percé to Pendleton it is all rolling farmlands, some of the fields left to grass and others planted in wheat and oats. On the highlands, though this was July, the hay crop was not yet cut, but as we moved down to Pendleton, the summer was further advanced and the hay in and the wheat ripening for what looked like a late August harvest.

Forgive these agricultural notes. I spent a lot of my boyhood on a farm in the south of England and developed, from my father, the habit of examining the state of crops wherever I go. He was a man who loved farming, and to hear him talk of vetches and silage and winter oats and rye grass was a cure for all the ailments of mankind. He would often stop the car when we were driving, climb some stranger's fence, walk about in his field and ruminate on the way the crop was growing, and he did this in England or Ireland or France or wherever he might be. Plants he loved but towards animals he showed respect but not affection. The sole exception was pigs. He believed in keeping pigs in the open and not in sties, and they loved him for it. We had a big field with many pigs in it, and when my father went through the gate he would in a moment be the center of a herd of grunting, adoring pigs. If you want to get along with a pig, by the way, poke it in the back with a stick, right around the short ribs.

The pig, I am told, is the most intelligent of the mammals, far ahead of the horse, the dog and the cat. I think it is

Gibbon who remarks that there are but two animals on earth who can thrive in the arctic cold and the tropic heat. One is Man and the other, the pig.

Well, I did not stop at Pendleton to buy a shirt or a blanket, but I did marvel at the change in vegetation that takes place about that little city. For we had come down from grassy plateaus and valleys, without a tree to be seen, to find Pendleton surrounded by trees, which seem to be protecting the town from the ocean of cornfields around. The crop was not all corn (by corn I mean oats—not Indian corn, which I am used to calling maize). There were also fields of wheat and of barley, with not a weed to be seen—no splash of red poppies or white flowers of cockle. I suppose weed killer has taken care of all that.

But my father would not have been happy over the size of the ears. They were small by his standards so the yield per acre would not have been lavish. On the other hand, this was Western America, not England. The yield per acre might be low but there were millions of acres available. I will tell you one more thing about my father, who was a professor of agriculture, and then leave him to his rest. He ran his whole life around this motto: "The rain that stops the reaper, starts the plough." I commend it to you in adversity and assure you that farming is but adversity overcome.

Well, here we were in Pendleton, down off the plateau, with its barley ripe for cutting though on the highlands the barley harvest was two months off. And at Pendleton before us was the Astor Party, following on the heels of Lewis and Clark and looking for the mouth of the Columbia. They found a river, then called the Eu-o-tah-la (modern Umatilla), "abounding with beaver," and they traded with the Indians for horses, which they ate. This was in the year 1812 when, on the Atlantic coast, the differences with England over the searching of ships had finally led to war—a surprising war which made the world's newest democracy, the United States, an ally of the world's newest tyranny—Napoleonic France. But we've seen some odd alliances in our time, too.

We climbed out of Pendleton towards Pilot Rock and passed through another of those invisible walls that separate one kind of country and vegetation from another. For from Walla Walla to Pendleton was all rich farmland. And then we came into the dry, sparse, semi-desert sort of country which looks like California. The hills were rounded and golden under their covering of grass, and over their tops hung a vast thunderstorm, purple as Concord grapes with shafts of pale sunlight striking down through it.

The storm moved down on us like the horde of Genghis Khan, preceded by outriders of seagulls, screeching and swooping about—the first we had seen since leaving Salt Lake City. Then the storm was upon us, bleak and cold, with walls of rain sweeping over the hill and the road and turning the windows of the bus into cataracts. There was a rumble or two of thunder and the breathless, scalding flash of lightning—both sheet lightning and forked lightning—and the tremendous noise and fury of it drowned out all other sounds.

At sea, sighting that purple front, I would long ago have made all secure and tucked a four-foot reef in the main. But I couldn't shorten sail on the bus. Gusts of wind smote it and drove it to leeward, for which the only cure was to reduce speed and step up the pace of the windshield wipers. The children became quiet and stared out of the windows, transported by this splendid storm from the trivial to the mighty in a matter of moments. And then it had gone off raging in the direction of Seattle. The sun came out again and the new-washed world glittered all about us.

We had been climbing all the time out of Pendleton's valley up what is called Franklin Hill, whose summit is nearly four thousand feet above sea level. The road down snaked in lovely coils through the basaltic lava of which the hill is composed. In parts this lay over a chalk stratum, meaning, I suppose, that the area was once marine, then rose perhaps, and the chalk was sealed off by lava flows from that vast range of volcanoes which once stood off the Pacific coast, and of which Washington's Mount Rainier is an outrider.

We were moving south now on Oregon Highway 395 on a return leg of our voyage. Let me recommend these smaller State highways to you, if you do not already know them. They are the antidote to the rush of time, and along them you will find more of America, its people and its history, than is available in the best library in the world. Here are farmhouses built a hundred years ago, built in the lovely haphazard way that shows the growth of a family from generation to generation here. You can study them and see how the original small building had first a pantry added, and then a living room separate from the kitchen, and then the kitchen was enlarged, and then a bigger dining room added and then a porch and so on. There are whole generations of families in these buildings, wholesome ordinary wonderful families whose sum total make the nation—a nation so strangely portrayed in terms of drug use and crime but actually deeply concerned with the decencies of living which brought it into being.

One such hamlet we came to and passed the night in. It is called Ione and its population is 301. I have a message for six young men of Ione. The message is this: That huge elm still stands in the center of the town, over sixty feet tall, I would say, grave and comforting and utterly overshadowing the frame house below with the gable windows and curlicues on the porch. The house is still painted white. On the road down to the school on the opposite side, the lady still has that bold wallpaper in her living room that everybody talked about when she put it up.

The crickets still sing in the evenings and you can hear the wind in the tops of the trees coming down from the golden hills that rise up beyond the town.

The children stay out playing until about nine o'clock and then they are rounded up and a hush descends on the streets.

The grade school is still there, at the end of the town. It's painted pink now. Right beside it there is laid out a new playing field—big enough for football or baseball. It is called the Ione Memorial Field, and as you enter it, there is a placard which says:

In Memoriam World War II

Tench Aldrich
Herbert Davidson
Alfred Emert
Clarence Harris
Bobbie Morgan
Paul Reitmann

November 11, 1948.

The town hasn't changed much since you went away. You'd find it about the same. Nobody's forgotten you either. The pain of your death is still there in some of the homes. . . .

chapter
Eighteen

THE state flower of Oregon should be, and perhaps it is, the foxglove. It grows abundantly along the hedges and by the roadside and even in whole gardens in the middle of fields, purple and white and often five feet tall. In my boyhood in the south of England I had always reckoned the foxglove a rare flower, found in boskier dells of woods, shy and full of witchery, for out of it, I was told, was obtained digitalis, which quickens the pace of the heart.

"The foxglove . . . is sparingly naturalized in North America," says the Britannica, ignorant of the hedgerows and ditches and fields of northern Oregon where it is in a fair way to oust the grass. It has a variety of names, being called in Ireland "fairy thimbles" and in Wales "elf's glove," and in Scotland "bloody fingers" and "dead-men's bells," pointing to a certain grimness in the Scots character. The French, by contrast, call it *doigts de la Vierge,* the Virgin's fingers, and the Germans called it *Fingerhut* which means thimble and it was this reference to finger that inspired the naturalist Fuchs, in 1542 or thereabouts, to give the name *digitalis* to the plant.

Whatever the farmer's viewpoint, it was pleasant to see whole swatches of foxgloves in the northern Oregon meadows and hedges, growing out of the basalt, which is characteristic of this region.

I wanted to see the Columbia River, however, and took the little State Highway 74 northward along Willow Creek, to its junction with the Columbia. A vast river it is at this point, entering a gorge which, deeply terraced, spoke of other depths of the river in eras long past. And Lord what a westerly swept up the Columbia to greet us as we turned onto Superhighway 80N and, with a pang of regret for the foxgloves and the little hamlet of Ione, headed for Portland. It was a fifty-knot blow and a headwind all the way, and raised wavelets capped with white on the Columbia even so far inland as we now were.

Even on the Superhighway I cut my speed to 50 miles an hour to cope with this wind, and several times, caught in gusts, was hard put to stop the bus being blown from one lane into another. This must be a land wind, however, for on that very day, a year previously, I had been at sea off that coast participating in the race from Vancouver to the Hawaiian Islands and in about the same latitude. My log spoke of light winds and flat calms and I could have done with that splendid westerly to send me speeding down to the tradewinds a thousand miles away.

We got lost in Portland, of course, for no city to my knowledge has yet devised roadsigns readily understood by strangers. The road builders of America are without peer in the world. But when it comes to wording signs which will give information clearly and quickly, they need to go back to school. A sign, for instance, which says:

80
North
West

even if it is contained in a most attractive shield, confuses me. I presume at first glance that I am traveling northwest on Highway 80. Hazel points out that I am on Highway 80 North, and traveling west, but this produces mental confusion because I immediately ask myself how could it be possible to travel west on a highway which goes north?

Lest it be thought that I am picking on Oregon here, let me say that I think California a very bad offender in the matter of road signs. There many of the freeways are named for cities—the San Diego freeway, for instance. Someone from out of state may be forgiven for assuming that the San Diego freeway goes to San Diego. And so it does in one direction but in the other direction it goes to San Francisco, so that there is no guarantee that in getting on the San Diego freeway you are going to reach San Diego. The Golden State freeway remains a mystery for me to this day. Whenever I get on it I know I am lost and salvation lies in getting off as soon as possible.

In the present case, having got onto Highway 80 North, which was headed west and not north at all, I had a very hard time getting onto State Highway 8, which would take me out to Tillamook, where the loveliest cheddar cheese in the world is to be had by the ton. We shot round and round in the center of Portland several times, rather like the ball in a pinball machine and finally, by listening carefully to Hazel and utterly ignoring my own directional instinct, we found Highway 8 and left Portland behind—happy to be headed back to the Pacific, which we had left ages and ages ago, it seemed.

Highway 8 climbs and twists over a range of mountains or perhaps they are only hills, towards the coast. It is a lovely road to drive on, well surfaced and going through forested country, mostly conifers. A man from Oregon, I am sure, would know larch from pine from fir from cedar from spruce, and given a little time I can separate some of these but I get lost in the pines for there seem so many of them.

In places, however, we went not through living forests but through the cemetries or graveyards of what were once splendid forests, areas of such destruction that they looked very much like the battlefields of the First World War with everything destroyed except where here and there a ragged stump reared up naked against the sky protesting the slaughter.

It is all necessary, we are told, but it is also horrible. We passed peaks which were entirely covered by the dead stumps of what were once splendid trees. Stripped of branches and bark there they stand with some kind of scrub growing around them which may or may not be the new forest that the lumber company planted to replace the one destroyed.

These are sharp peaks, cones almost, rather than the rounded hills of California, so there are steep gulleys between them. And lying in these, like so many jackstraws, were scores of dead trees, which might be fetched out later for the pulp mill or left to rot where they were.

Some peaks were utterly denuded of all growth. The broken rock, of a shade between blue and brown, lies open to the ravages of the sun and of rain, being eroded at ten times the natural rate. The paper and lumber companies spend a lot of money in advertising showing how they are replacing logged-out forests with new ones which one is led to believe will be even better than the old and of which the animals will be even fonder. But Highway 8 and the coast highway south for many miles give the lie to those advertisements. There are the slaughtered forests in all their gaunt death, and without looking at the map you can tell when you enter a State or National Park, for suddenly the trees are healthy and lush and strong, contrasting with the battlefield sections where logging has been permitted.

I do not want to be unfair to the lumber and paper companies. Their work is essential and their product in great demand. I do wonder, however, whether that widespread destruction of trees, which seem to be wasted in a large part, is necessary. And whose trees are they? I wonder. Yours and mine, perhaps, like the air and the sea and the river? If so we should certainly have a say on the extent to which they are to be cut and the rate at which they are to be replaced.

What made this wood wastage seem all the more extravagant was the enormous number of logs which we found choking every bay and inlet on the Oregon coast when we got there. Not thousands but millions of board feet of wood, littering every bay and surely of use in paper making if not in construction. It seems easier to cut down more trees than to salvage those which have drifted away. I must confess the wastage seemed the greater to me because I have to pay sixty dollars a cord for firewood; mostly scrub oak and eucalyptus.

The lushness of the Oregon forests is almost tropical. Moss grows inches thick on the branches of pine trees, and those Oregon pines are among the noblest. Four logs made a full load for a semi-trailer of great size, and some of the standing trees seemed a hundred feet high. The lushness is reflected in the roadside flowers, Queen Anne's Lace, foxgloves, dill, and at one place a veritable thicket of wild sweet peas, so lovely that I stopped the bus so we could all get out and enjoy them. The fruit or seed of dill is used as a condiment and the leaves were once used in making a kind of soup called dilligrout. The Lords of the Manor of Addington in Surrey, England, held their title in return for supplying a dish of dilligrout to the king (or queen) at the coronation banquet. However a coronation banquet has not been held in over a century in Britain, so no dilligrout has been called for in many generations. It isn't something I would rush out to prepare. Charles II, who had spent his youth as a wanderer around European courts and had a strong stomach as a result, had some dilligrout at his coronation banquet, ate but one spoonful and announced emphatically that he didn't like it.

We were disappointed in not finding the whole of Tillamook full of cheese. I know I have already remarked that it is bootless to search for coal in Newcastle, so I should not have been surprised at not finding that excellent cheddar for which it is famous in Tillamook. But the fact is that ages before—well, at least in the pre-atomic age—we drove through Tillamook and found lots of cheese and bought several pounds and the sharp but creamy flavor lingered with us ever afterward.

Tillamook has changed since then, however. The main road through it is vast and thronged with traffic, or was on this second visit, and not only could we find no cheese but we could find no place to empty that terrible tank which required once again to be vented of its azure tide.

I cannot remember exactly when we sighted the sea or rather the ocean. We were all looking forward to it, of course, for the children have lived all their lives within sight of the Pacific and they missed it. But we topped a rise somewhere and there it lay, pearl gray, calm, immense, and inviting. We didn't cheer. We just stopped the bus and looked at it, each feeling his own satisfaction and fulfillment that we were back close to it after thousands of miles of desert and mountain travel. That wind which we had met in traveling the course of the Columbia is a canyon wind, by the way. Once we left the river the wind was gone and it did not blow over the ocean, whose great surface was undisturbed except for a slow and easy rise and fall—the remnant, perhaps, of a storm over by the coast of Japan.

Cheeseless, we left Tillamook and headed south on the Pacific Coast Highway, looking for a place to park for the night. The day was overcast, and heavy clouds rolled up from the southwest, threatening rain which did not materialize. I did not want to travel in the rain with dark approaching. I made up my mind to stop early. And yet the forests (when not logged) were so verdant and lovely and the little bays to our right such a delight that I could not resist the temptation to go on mile after mile, filled with pleasure at the magnificent Oregon coastline. I am prepared to proclaim the Oregon coast superior to any other in the world. I am prepared to declare its ocean cleaner and smoother, its rocks rockier, its bays cozier and its sands smoother than are to be found in any other known part of the earth from Ambrose Light to west or east of Krakatoa, which ever takes your fancy. To be sure I have not visited all these coasts, but one does not have to know that they could not outshine the lovely bays and cliffs of Oregon. I have a suspicion, however, that the ocean off Oregon is cold enough to cut glass, for I did not see a single person swimming or riding the lovely surf, which in days to come will, I am sure, be one of the greatest of Oregon's attractions. Having paid this handsome and entirely justified compliment to Oregon, I still think it is a pity that we could not get any cheese in Tillamook.

The scenery was, however, so entrancing that I passed

trailer park after trailer park and when we did stop, I found that we had covered three hundred and eighty miles in that day. Far, far too much. But who is going to grumble about three hundred and eighty miles of forest and flowers and ferns and pearl-gray seas and bays and cliffs straight out of a Chinese painting?

We sang on the latter stage of our journey and pulled into the Siltcoos National Park, where we found a space to stay for the night. There was still an hour or two of daylight and the threat of rain had gone as we gained southing. Out jumped the children and the kitten as soon as the bus had stopped and went off to explore sand dunes and copse and a little creek that led down to the sea. We dined sumptuously on beans and wieners and, the adventures of *The Hobbit* being finished, the children beat me at cards once more before retiring for the night.

chapter

Nineteen

UP TO this point we had traveled over three thousand miles through the American West, passing through the states of California, Arizona, Utah, Colorado, Montana, Idaho, Wyoming, Washington, and now Oregon. One impression, perhaps the strongest of the whole voyage, was how empty the land is. This, of course, led to the speculation that people who get anxious about the population explosion might relieve their tensions by getting out of the big cities and traveling about the land. With ten times our present population it would still be empty. The population explosion is not evident in the country. It is to be found only in the big cities, which attract more and more people from the country, both for the ease of earning a better livelihood and for the convenience of central heating, public transportation, theaters, restaurants and so on.

The wilderness and the semi-wilderness is still there, immense and nourishing for both spirit and body. Solitude is not more than two hours' drive from the center of any city in the United States. In two hundred years it may be three hours' drive. Or then again, in two hundred years, we may have faster cars and it may be only fifteen minutes from Broadway to bird song.

The little towns are, of course, just holding their own, or dying as the big cities thrive. The younger generation moves off and the town is left to the old folks. Washington and Oregon are full of lovely small towns—really small with a population of a few hundred. The houses are old and have the kind of luxuriant gardens you see in jigsaw puzzle pictures. There is moss on the roofs and the fences want a bit of repairing. You could perhaps buy one of those houses—wonderful homes—for about half of what you would pay for a house in a modern suburb, and get with it more ground than you can take care of. But in these rural places it is hard to earn a living, and it certainly seems that the cities are bound to grow and the countryside is bound to get emptier and emptier. The logical conclusion of the process might be a nation of one thousand or more great cities surrounded by almost empty countryside. Goldsmith's *Deserted Village,* which applied to England in the eighteenth century, applies to America in the twentieth.

Bandon, Oregon, is one of the little towns where you may meet a deer in your back garden. It lies in the middle of Oregon's myrtle belt—a tract on the Oregon coast where the myrtle grows (it is alleged to grow nowhere else) and where you can pick up lovely articles like candlesticks and salad bowls made of gold and black wood. We stopped at Mr. Zumwalt's shop right on the highway to look for things in this lovely wood, and I tried to recall Marlowe's poem "The Passionate Shepherd to His Love" which contains some lines about myrtle. But my memory rarely works on demand and the more insistent the demand the less likely that it will work.

So going into Mr. Zumwalt's myrtle shop I could not remember Marlowe's words about myrtle, but I have since looked them up and they are as follows:

> "And I will make thee beds of roses
> And a thousand fragrant posies,
> A cap of flowers, and a kirtle,
> Embroidered all with leaves of myrtle."

Mr. Zumwalt didn't have any myrtle leaves, but he had a lovely display of turned, polished and carved myrtle wood—salad spoons, bowls, forks, candlesticks, book ends, place settings, pen stands—just about everything that can be made in wood. The wood is the most delightful in the world. I have said black and gold but actually it is a very deep brown in splotches set off against a light gold sapwood. Not even the maple backs of the best violins can match the loveliness of this cypress and this thought prompted me to ask Mr. Zumwalt whether anybody had ever made a violin with a myrtle back.

"Yes," he said. "I knew a fellow who gave up wood carving to make fiddles with myrtle backs. He made about twenty of them and they were the prettiest things you ever saw. But the tone was terrible and in a few months they had all warped out of shape and were useless." He had a call, he said, for "fiddleback maple"—that is, maple with a lovely curl to the veining—and sold it to dealers in San Fancisco. There used to be a man who came by once a year or so looking for maples for violins but he had not seen him in some time and thought he might be ill.

Mr. Zumwalt had been a wood carver, specializing in myrtle, for over a quarter of a century in that one place. His workshop was right behind his store and he designed everything that he sold himself. It was all beautiful. It was the kind of merchandise you can only buy in the most expensive stores in large cities and then you have to pay big sums. He did a big trade, he said, in myrtle for gunstocks and showed us some which were very handsome. We also saw the workshop with its piles of shavings and neat little mounds of the loveliest smelling sawdust.

There is about woodworking shops—carpenter shops, I used to call them—a steadiness very soothing to the mind. I lived at one time in a village in the south of England called Crawley and spent some of my happiest hours in the village carpenter's shop. He repaired all the wagons drawn by those horses that taught me to swear and indeed he made the carts, wheels and all, though when a wheel was made it was sent up to the blacksmith at the top of the village to have a red-hot iron tire shrunk onto it. The process was to heat the iron tire, drop it around the wooden wheel and then throw water on it, whereupon it shrank and pulled the wheel together. I only saw this done once and I doubt it is done at all now. The blacksmith made all the shoes for the horses and I watched him do that often enough, fashioning a shoe out of a piece of strip iron in a matter of minutes. The shoes were put on hot so they would bed well in the hoof, I suppose, and it filled me with anxiety as a boy to smell the burning hoof when the hot shoe was put on, though the horses themselves seemed indifferent, merely twitching their skin here and there, the cleverest way, to get rid of flies. This blacksmith could hold a six-pound sledgehammer in one hand at arm's length, and the dark interior of his forge was covered with colored postcards, designed by some descendant of Rabelais, I fancy.

The carpenter in the village had a very pleasant smell

about him, which I later learned was beer. He drank heavily and people despised him for this. But to return to Mr. Zumwalt. He told me he had forty years of woodworking behind him and maybe more. He had spent his whole life in the trade and found content in it too. The myrtle groves, he said, are found in three counties on the coast of Oregon and extend eighty miles inland.

In the southern portion of Oregon and in places where the undergrowth has been cut away, the sand dunes are marching inland and submerging the coastal forests. We came to one such place where, with the undergrowth stripped off, the sand, driven before the westerly winds, had built dunes a third and more up the trunks of tall pines. These were dying, falling askew, and the victorious sand had pushed across the highway to the forest on the inland side.

This is a perfect example of desert—sand desert—in the making and it is a serious matter, for some of the world's most luxuriant countries have been reduced to wilderness by this very process. In early Roman times, for instance, North Africa was a heavily wooded area. It was in this forested and fertile region that Horace, the poet, lived and at one time it was possible to ride from Tripoli to the Atlantic entirely under the shade of vast trees. The deep forests of Tunis supplied the wild beast for the Roman arenas.

Now all this region is reduced to desert as a result of the cutting down of the underbrush which permitted the wind, piling up sand, to gradually bury and destroy these magnificent forests.

North Africa is not unique. The Syrian desert was once very heavily populated—a fertile and pleasant land producing many fruits, including apples. Today it is almost without life. Palmyra was a city named for its flourishing palms.

It is now a huddle of miserable houses in a barren land, and what of Babylon's Ur? That great city that once occupied an area of four square miles and had a population of half a million was destroyed by wind and dust storms as the forests around were cut down and the shrubs grazed out. The dust storms still rage there and at times for six weeks on end the sun is only a pale thin wafer in the murky sky.

So wind and sand, aided by man's carelessness, have buried and turned to desert some of the loveliest places on earth. And in places the pines of southern Oregon are being killed by marching sand dunes. The process of desert-making is aided by the logging of trees and it is almost terrifying to see the gaunt survivors, standing stripped of leaves and of bark, looking about affrighted at what happened to their companions.

I suppose there are redwoods in Oregon but we did not see any. However, we were no sooner across the California line than there they were, the first of these magnificent trees which are the tallest in the world, the oldest in the world, and certainly the most famous in the world. They soar upward one hundred, two hundred, three hundred feet. They are absolutely impossible to photograph and they are not to be described except with plentiful reference to cathedrals, for they have the same solemn dignity, the same loftiness, the same sense of communication with the Creator, the same silence, the same endurance and the same peace.

You are aware, of course, that you can drive a car through some of the redwoods and that there is in one of these gigantic trees sufficient timber for forty houses, and that when Columbus reached the Americas, many of the trees now standing were full grown. But being aware of these things does not in the slightest degree prepare you for their presence. They are to botany what the Grand Canyon is to geology; giant-sized and magnificent and having definite personality so that they are not objects but beings and one talks in their presence in lowered tones.

We took the Redwood Highway and the Avenue of the Giants through these tremendous groves. And we stopped again and again to leave the bus and walk into the forest among the lovely ferns, which were as high as ourselves, in the air stained green by the vegetation, to see the lofty columns of the trees soaring to the skies and the graceful shafts of sunlight striking down to the ground. The sunlight makes the soft reddish-brown bark of the trees glow where it touches and because of the contrast of the surrounding shadows gives a glow also to fern and bramble and the other undergrowth. It is strange that upon reflection I cannot recall hearing a single bird call among those mighty redwoods. It was as if all other senses were suspended and sight only remained.

That the redwoods survive is a triumph of man's reverence over man's cupidity. For there was a time when these mighty groves were in danger of destruction by the lumber interests, who still have envious eyes on those board feet of timber. These preserved forests are forests from the youth of the world before man or industry came to change and to destroy. The trees are perfectly straight and where one has been cut another grows out of the stump, for the redwood has an enormous capacity for life and has for this reason been given the name *Sequoia sempervirens*. This ability to produce what are called "coppice sprouts" is common among broadleafed trees, but rare among conifers, but the redwood owes much of its longevity to its resistance to fire and I think to insect pests.

The enormous thick and moist bark forms a wonderful insulation against flame, and redwoods which have been severely burned on the interior (perhaps by lightning) still flourish, though charred and hollow for perhaps forty feet of their height above the ground.

I had better say here and now that there are two kinds of redwood. There is the coastal species, which grows the tallest and is called, as I have said, *Sequoia sempervirens,* and then there is another inland species, discovered in 1850 in the Sierra Nevada, which have much bigger boles but do not grow quite so high. These are called *Sequoia gigantea.* A third species, called Dawn redwoods, was found about twenty years ago in a valley in China and it is believed that these are the trees from which the California redwoods descend. That species, however, is extinct in California and I believe everywhere in the world but in the Chinese valley where they were discovered. A few, I am told, are being raised from seed in the United States.

One of the odd things about the redwood tree is that, despite its tremendous height, it has no tap root. Its roots are spread fanlike close to the surface, and as a result the tree is in the gravest danger of toppling over if it gets even the slightest bit out of the perpendicular. To overcome this, the trees perform a very careful balancing act. The slightest tendency to lean one way is compensated by the growing of a branch on the opposing side, the branch being nicely calculated to be of such a size as to compensate for the leaning. Some of the redwoods have been balancing for centuries, and at this point I begin to wonder what is "intelligence" and whether "intelligence" is possessed by vegetation. If intelligence consists in sensing a peril and taking the steps needed to avoid it, then redwoods are intelligent beings.

I will cite you also the example of trees which hunt for their food, though not the man-eating trees of Madagascar, which flourished in the Sunday supplements of my youth and nowhere else. There is, for example, a kind of tree in the tropics (I met it in Trinidad, British West Indies) which is called boxwood and which produces a nut which splits with great force, ejecting the seed. The seeds, to flourish, require quantities of phosphorus and these trees grow along the banks of rivers. The seed ejected into the stream gives off strychnine which kills fish which, decomposing in the area, provide the needed phosphorus for both the parent tree and the seeds.

I cannot give you this as a matter of scientific fact for I am not a botanist. I am, however, witness to the explosion of the nut containing the seed, and the velocity with which the seed is expelled. But there is also in the tropics a kind of ground cover related to mimosa and this catches flies, the tiny leaves closing as soon as touched by an insect. The mimosa moreover had the ability to learn. You may touch it twice with your finger and it will close. But touch it a third time and it refuses to be fooled, having learned that no food is offered and there is no sense responding. This is more intelligence than is displayed by many dogs, who will come time and again for food if you only rattle their feeding bowl. Or maybe dogs are optimists whereas plants are pessimists.

Since plants have not the nervous system of animals it is assumed that they do not feel pain. Yet the reaction of the mimosa touched shows that some plants at least have a tactile sense and it is disturbing to think, viewing a bouquet of roses in one's living room, that they may all be screaming. Hazel believes that plants respond to affection and they certainly respond very well to her. She can produce much better

chapter Twenty

WE STOPPED at Leggett that night in a lovely State Park, lodging the bus among big trees, with birds all about the soft mold of leaves and twigs underfoot. We had been doing too much mileage, enticed to go farther and farther by the excitement and loveliness of the scenery, which like life itself, promised always something even better around the next bend.

My family and I are gypsies to a degree, taking our delight in movement more than in rest, in change rather than in the familiar. We will stop for an hour or two in some redwood grove or by some beach of breathlessly white sand. But then we must move on to see whatever lies beyond the bend and we do not need, in traveling thus, any more amusement than to be able to look out at the scenery, whether of earth or of sky.

I think that that State Park at Leggett must be one of the most peaceful places on earth, though it is very close to Highway 101. The trees absorb the automobile noise entirely, the air is soft and cool and the sunlight has the glow and spangle of life to it. In the silence all the delightful forest sounds are to be heard, the hushing of the wind through the upper branches and even the distinct and neat sound which a twig makes in falling to the earth.

You can almost hear each leaf stir in the breeze, and the forest aroma of mold and of sap and ferns revitalizes your lungs. Some people are afraid of forests and Hazel, brought up in the high desert of Arizona, is not overly fond of trees. She does not dislike them, but after a while they make her melancholy and she longs for wide desert and the hard glinting sun and purple mountains. But I feel safer in forests than anywhere else on earth and if any great calamity were to overtake the nation, I think I would run to the forests for safety and comfort.

That is odd really because in Ireland, where I was born, there are no forests. All the great trees were logged out to provide ships for our enemy's navy though at one time great forests covered the land and abounded in red deer and elk. The remnants of these trees are to be found in the bogs of central and western Ireland and are called "bog oak" though they are not oak at all, but pine and cedar and yew, I think. It would seem, looking at the rings on these ancient trees, that when they went the climate changed, for the rings indicate many years of drought whereas in the same area now over a hundred inches of rain will fall in a year.

We had a very pleasant time of it at Leggett and, the following day, deserted Highway 101 for a while to get once more to the ocean, for the highway had passed inland through the redwoods.

The bus had been behaving beautifully apart from that trouble with the starter which I could now live with. We found a road headed to State Highway 1, which follows the

California coast, and took it and immediately ran into trouble. The road was cut into the side of mountains between us and the coast. It had washed out in places in the tempestuous rains of spring. We snaked upward and upward, with a mountain wall on one side and a sheer drop on the other, and as we climbed the weather thickened and soon there were patches of heavy mist.

Then the transmission started to complain. It felt hot and smelled and I feared that it was low on fluid. No gasoline stations were to be found, of course, so we crawled up and up, sometimes stopping to cool off the transmission and sometimes having to back up a bit to let an oncoming camper by. I hate to make a sick engine work but there was no help for it. Everytime I put the engine in gear or changed down, I suffered agonies for that transmission and when at last we got to the peak of the mountain range and could look forward to going down there was no real relief for us.

The engine did not labor, of course, but the brakes took heavy punishment, and after a while got that hard feeling which meant that they were overheated and likely to "fade." The smell of burning brake lining was soon strong and the road merciless. Having ascended to the heavens at a tremendous pitch, it now plunged towards sea level at the same angle.

I set up the hand brake to its maximum to help the foot brake and transferred some of the braking load to the transmission by dropping down to low at the steeper parts. So for a while we had this smell of overheated transmission and overheated brakes in the bus. The hairpin bends and dog legs, of which there were plenty, were the worst, for if the brakes gave out in negotiating them there was a good chance of plunging over the cliff. We were an hour and a half getting from Leggett to Rockport though the distance is under thirty miles; and at Rockport, on the coast, could find no gas station and found none until we got to Fort Bragg, where we received succour at last.

There is beyond Fort Bragg a tiny little town of great charm called Noyo, where everybody in the world ought to be allowed to spend a few weeks to compensate for a lifetime of taxation, imposts, form filling, paper filing, magazine reading, and telephones. It is a jewel of a place in a little dell, with a river running through and a road by the river and a shipyard where two fine fishing vessels of perhaps fifty tons were being built side by side of steel. Noyo has gardens and sunshine and a drawling air, and out beyond, at the end of the bay, is the tremendous ocean, green and blue and vigorous in the westerly winds.

The day we were there a man in cowboy boots, jeans, and a ten-gallon hat walked awkwardly along the main street carrying freshly caught salmon, and I was reminded somehow of the story of how they caught the salmon in the policeman's hat in Stephens' *Crock of Gold.*

I do not know what was the matter with the transmission. When we got to the flatland it worked perfectly, and the level of the fluid was, on examination, what it should have been. Perhaps the steep grades of the mountain road piled the fluid at one end of the case and so caused our difficulty.

Traveling towards San Francisco and being still on the coast road, we saw at "Ten Mile River," between Westport and Fort Bragg, how the sand had drifted before the west wind over the river and dunes of sand were marching through a grove of eucalyptus whose staggered trunks lay dying in the clutch of the newly born desert. Already farms in this area are being deserted, for when a certain portion of sand becomes mixed with soil, the soil is sterile and will not even produce good grazing. The damage at present is not extensive. But it is like the beginning of a cancer. Checked now a lovely countryside may be saved. Ignored, its death is assured.

This was the Fourth of July weekend and the Coast Highway was soon too heavily congested for pleasure and so we went inland back to Highway 101 through those same coastal mountains which had caused me so much anxiety on their first crossing. But heading for Ukiah the grades were more gentle and gave us little trouble. And at Ukiah we passed through another invisible wall. Somewhere in that region, we traveled from Anglo-Saxon America into Spanish-America. Names like Newport, Fort Bragg, and Willitts were left behind and replaced by names which formed a litany of all the saints—San Jose, Santa Rosa, San Francisco, Santa Clara, and so on.

What a vast empire the Spanish built in their great days! It extended from California to Cape Horn and from there westward to the Philippines and again from Cape Horn eastward to Africa, where it has its remnant in the island of Fernando Po in the Guinea Gulf of Africa. These were a mighty people whom we, with our Anglo-Saxon heritage, have ignored for did we not beat their Armada in 1588 and beat them again at San Juan Hill (when they were not looking) in 1901? But what a heritage of glory they left, these Spanish, Cortez taking Mexico with his handful; Pizarro, Peru; Cabazo de Vaca exploring in Louisiana and up the Mississippi Valley; Portola leading his band in Revolutionary times up the California coast. It does not belittle us to acknowledge how great they were.

Take a look at the globe and think of the galleon voyage from Manila to the Panama Isthmus. It was an argosy itself over thousands of miles of uncharted ocean. Think then of transshipping the cargoes of those galleons and transporting them across the Isthmus on muleback through countryside that quelled Morgan's starving horde a century later. Think of those cargoes being transshipped again at Vera Cruz or Nombre de Dios for the second ocean voyage, this time across the Atlantic, skirting Florida's treacherous reefs and the terrible Bermudas, and arriving at Spain. Five years of a man's life could be spent on such a voyage and many did not survive it. But such a tremendous journey did not quell the Spanish and I say, however much we have mocked at their lumbering galleons in the Armada fight, they were the world's most daring seamen in their day and walked the oceans as readily as they did the highways of Castile.

They were destroyed not by their enemies but by their own aristocracy. Many a Spanish seaman must have cursed the folly that put as admiral of a fleet a duke who had never seen ocean water. England's naval might lay in the fact that her great captains came out of the forecastle or, at least, the midshipman's cuddy. And Spain's downfall lay in the fact that her captains came from the castles of Leon and Aragon and Castile. Her seamen never failed her.

It is said, on the other hand, that the Spanish were cruel and indeed it is a universal opinion that this was so. They cut off the hands of the Indians and cut out their tongues and piled their severed limbs at corners of a trail in their colonies as a warning to others. They used fire and the stake and the lash to make converts of the poor redmen.

How odd then to see that in the Spanish countries the Indians thrived and are still the major element of the population. By contrast in the non-Spanish territories, the Indians have either been killed off or live as a remnant on a reservation. How does one explain that? How many of the Seneca are there in New England, or of Sioux in Wyoming? But the Indian population of Mexico is huge and so also of Bolivia and Chile and Argentina. I give you these thoughts for your deliberations and to them add one other—no nation is glorious whose history is written by its enemies. We of Ireland know that well.

We had then, a little south of Ukiah, entered the ghost of that vast Spanish Empire which was greater than that of Rome, and that we had done so was evident in more than names. The crops also changed, for south of Ukiah you will find some of the best of California's vineyards, of which some of the best lie in the Napa Valley. The verdant redwoods petered out, though I am aware that there are groves farther south at Muir Woods and also at Santa Cruz, and the Mediterranean climate started to assert itself. Peaches and almonds appeared though you must clear San Francisco by two hundred miles southing, I think, before you will come on oranges. Talking then of the glories of Spain we headed for Monterey, where in my innocence I had set my heart on a fish dinner on the pier within sight of the lovely Monterey fishing boats whose graceful bows come direct, I am sure, from ancient Phoenicia and were known to the sailors of long lost Tarshish.

chapter

Twenty-one

THE decision to get a fish dinner at Monterey was one of the worst of the whole voyage, readily outclassing that other decision to cross Death Valley in the height of the summer. For Monterey has become famous, nationally and internationally. And this being the Fourth of July there were more people pouring into Monterey than into downtown New York on a Monday morning.

It was overwhelming. There was a deluge of them and the nearer I got to the pier area the more like Coney Island the whole thing became. Three streets from the waterfront, the roads had been taken over by pedestrians, and we inched through them in the bus feeling worse and worse about the whole thing until finally we decided that sanity could be preserved only by getting out again.

Now, here is a mystery. Everyone to whom I have spoken on the subject hates crowds, and my experience to date is that all human beings are crowd-haters. Why is it then that at every holiday people crowd together as if the whole object of the holiday was to get as close as possible to as many people as possible? Are crowds composed of crowd-haters? And if this is so, is not this one of the strangest contradictions in the whole of Nature?

Overwhelmed and surrounded by this tide of our fellow creatures, we searched for a place in which to turn the bus around and flee down the highway as fast as we could from Monterey.

One big attraction for the crowd, I am sure, was the promise of the Navy to have a rocket display from warships off shore. Another may be the fame attaching to Monterey as a result of the writing of Steinbeck. Another may have been the natural beauty of the place, for there are few towns with so delightful a bay fronting them though I hear that that bay is now so polluted that it is dangerous to swim in it. Still it looks lovely, with the dark cedars on the spit of land to the north, and the colorful pier, with its splashes of orange and white and blue, thrusting out over what were clear waters.

I was disappointed not to get my fish dinner at Monterey, where the lobster and crab are excellent and the deep sea scallops fit for Poseidon himself. My faith persuades me to eat fish on Fridays, but this is done for the mortification of the flesh and I have at sea received many singular signs that the Lord takes this matter seriously in my case. Once, on a Friday, heading up the California coast close-hauled in a brisk northwesterly, I told Kevin to take the wheel while I went below to fix a sandwich or two for dinner.

"It's Friday, Dad," said Kevin, seeing me opening a can of deviled ham.

"So it is," I said. "And Mother Church has wisely ordained that those upon the sea may eat meat on a Friday, the better to sustain themselves against the perils of the deep. Fall off a touch, if you will, please, for I feel the jib backing."

So I went on and fixed my deviled ham sandwiches and I had hardly taken a bite of one before my peak halyard parted, flinging the mainsail into a welter of canvas with the heavy gaff threatening to brain anyone who came within a foot of it.

On another occasion, having once more pointed out to Hazel that wise provision permitting seamen to eat meat on Fridays, I concluded with the words, "Furthermore, if the Lord wished me to eat fish, he would send me one, for we are at sea and there are a ton and a half of them without a doubt within a few feet of this boat." Hardly were the words out of my mouth before a flying fish of a pound and a half leaped out of the water and fell upon the foredeck. I did not, to be sure, eat this, my fellow creature, who was merely carrying out the orders of his Creator, but returned him to the sea and made my dinner of a can of sardines.

With this and other equally remarkable instances to point to, you may be sure that I eat fish on Fridays and would continue to do so even if the College of Cardinals were to absolve me from the duty in solemn conclave. But I do not like to eat fish on Fridays and therein is the virtue of the whole thing, for we improve ourselves largely by doing things that we do not like to do—a solemn truth which I recommend to the younger generation about me.

However, fish on the pier at Monterey, or in the fine fish restaurant on Third Avenue in New York called, I do believe, The King of the Sea, or at the Cafe Royal in London, where they served a sole *bonne femme* that was a credit to all mankind; such fish is no mortification at all and I adore it. It is just Friday fish that I do not like so I was as I say sorry to miss my fish dinner at Monterey and set off muttering hard words about Steinbeck, whom at the moment I held responsible for my disappointment.

I cannot now remember where we dined that day or what we dined on and it does not much matter. I think we stopped at one of those restaurants where you serve yourself and pay at the end—wonderful eating places they are, too, and if you should feel inclined to criticize them, I recommend you reflect on the situation in other countries. The hungriest road in the world, I do believe, is in Ireland and leads from Galway to Dublin. To be sure you can drive it in a matter of three hours or so but there is hardly a restaurant to be found on the way.

We were now overtaken by the homing urge. We were perhaps two hundred miles from Hermosa Beach or five hours' driving, and the sensible thing would have been to find a nice parking place for the night and finish the journey on the morrow. But everybody wanted to see our own home again as soon as possible; to open the front door and feel our own walls about us, and find how Rascal, our dog, was doing, and be consoled by the familiar drip of the faucet in the kitchen which I had not fixed all year.

I did dutifully suggest that we might stop and look for a parking place and I was met by silence as cool as a snowdrift. And then I said we could push on and get home, though it would be in the wee hours of the morning, and everybody perked up immediately.

So push on we did. Coco, Rory, Arabella and Tricia went to bed as the bus rolled through the night, but I could not get Hazel to go to bed. She sat in the copilot's seat and dozed a little while I rather enjoyed myself. It was like the night watch at sea; the lovely feeling of being alone in the wind and the dark and of owning yourself and having all the world at your disposal.

And so I drove on and on, down that mighty highway which is called 101 and is greater than anything the Romans ever built and leads, rightly viewed, from Canada to Mexico. The names of the towns became more familiar—the lovely ringing Spanish names of men unashamed of their faith—San Lucas, San Miguel, San Luis Obispo, Santa Maria, Santa Barbara. (Pray what have they called those great craters and peaks on the moon—is there not one named for God or His Holy Trinity?) And so finally to Santa Monica and Hermosa Beach.

It was indeed in the wee hours of the morning that, the voyage over, I pulled up alongside our house, parting with the top of the bus the boughs of those trees which we had parted on leaving, and turned off the engine and the headlights. Then I woke up the children and got them into the house and into their beds and quieted down Rascal, who was being cared for by a neighbor and had nearly gone out of her mind with joy at our return.

Kevin and Christopher were home asleep and merely grunted their welcome and turned over in their beds. When I had gone all around the house and touched everything to be sure it was the same, rather like a dog returning to his kennel, I went to bed myself.

And just as I was falling asleep I remembered that I never had emptied that tank of its azure piny fragrance and the thought of it troubled my dreams for the rest of the night.

ABOUT THE AUTHOR

Leonard Wibberley was born in Dublin, Ireland, in 1915. When he was nine, his family moved to England, settling in London. After the death of his father, a professor of agriculture, Mr. Wibberley went to work at the age of sixteen, first as a stockroom apprentice for a publisher and then as a reporter.

During the Depression, Mr. Wibberley suddenly left his newspaper job and, taking a violin, toured the northern counties of England playing in the streets. He did this, he says, "because I had a desire to be free of employment and also because I was nervous about losing a job with some eight millions out of work. The solution as I saw it was to quit, and having discovered that I could earn a reasonable living as a street musician, I was never much concerned about losing a job thereafter." (He still plays the violin for recreation.)

After this experience, he worked at various jobs, including stints as oil refinery operator and safety engineer. In 1943 he came to the United States where he went again into newspaper work, which occupied him for about ten years. He then decided to devote himself full time to writing.

Mr. Wibberley lives in Hermosa Beach, California, with his wife and six children. He is the author of numerous books, including many juveniles. He is best known for *The Mouse That Roared* and its successors, *The Mouse on the Moon* and *The Mouse on Wall Street*, published by Morrow in 1962 and 1969, respectively. *A Feast of Freedom*, published in 1964, received the annual award of the Southern California Council on Literature for Children and Young People.